Power Drinks

D1299265

Born in Berlin, in Germany, Catja Gramberg-Peklivanas has been interested in nutrition all her life having watched her older sister try out diet after diet in order to loose weight. An advocate of juicing for a number of years, she is always trying out new recipes on herself and her husband. Catja has a degree in Business Studies and is a qualified massage therapist. She is currently studying for an ITEC in Nutrition.

This is a Carlton Book

Copyright © Carlton Books Limited 2002

1 3 5 7 9 10 8 6 4 2

A CIP catalogue for this book is available from the British Library.

UK ISBN: 1 84222 671 1

US ISBN: 1 84222 569 3

Executive Editor: Vanessa Daubney

Project Art Direction: Darren Jordan

Production: Lisa French

Jacket Design: Mark Lloyd & Steve Lynn

Photography by Julian Hawkins

Printed and bound in Dubai

Power Drinks

Natural energy in a glass

Catja Gramberg-Peklivanas

CARLTON BOOKS

Contents

Introduction 5

A–Z of Fruit 6

A–Z of Vegetables 14

The Things You Don't See –
Antioxidants, Phytochemicals,
Vitamins, Minerals 24

Supplements 33

Additives 35

Preparing to Juice 37

Recipes – Feeling and Looking
Beautiful, Energy Elixirs, For
Women, For Men, For Children
and Young Adults, Under the
Weather, Let Your Hair Down 39

Conditions and Juices to Take 122

Equipment 128

Introduction

In today's fast-moving society, we tend to subject ourselves to high levels of stress in our day-to-day lives and we eat quite a poor variety of food, a lot of which is processed. This often leads to a deficiency in essential nutrients. But a fresh juice a day is a quick and effective way to feed our bodies with the vital vitamins and minerals our bodies need for optimum heath and vitality.

The process extracts the fibre of the fruits or vegetables, leaving all the nutrients in the juice, and because our bodies don't use a lot of energy to break down foods in this way, they absorb the nutrients far more quickly. So, this process can be particularly beneficial in cases where the body is weakened due to illness or old age.

The idea of this book is to provide the reader with a number of easy-to-follow recipes, which can help with common ailments and also help as pick-me-ups when you are feeling low. Some of the recipes contain supplements which act as a booster in one way or another but, if you like, you can add whatever supplement you feel you need to any of the other recipes and there is a list of supplements giving advice on how they work on page 33. But you will also see that each recipe list details of all the vitamins and minerals to be found in the ingredients.

Firstly, though, there are sections on fruit, vegetables and herbs and how they can be used, plus tables explaining the benefits of vitamins and minerals. These will give you some idea of the variety of food which is available and I hope act as an incentive to get you experimenting in making your own concoctions. And at the end of the book you will find a list of ailments and suggested recipes to try to alleviate some of the symptoms and advice on how to choose a good juicer and blender.

The important thing is to have fun when you make these recipes and to be inventive in creating your own. It's a great way to get a healthy body and mind.

Fruit and Vegetables

A good diet should contain at least five portions of fruit and vegetables every day to give our bodies adequate amounts of vital vitamins and minerals. However, it's often difficult to fit all these portions of fruit and vegetable into our busy daily lives, which is why juicing can help.

Raw foods have very high amounts of vitamins, minerals and enzymes, which are lost during cooking. Research has shown that certain fruits and vegetables in their raw state contain enzymes, which can fight many of today's illnesses. Carrots, for example, contain a fighter-preventative enzyme and raw carrot juice is now given to people with cancer to help the body fight cancer cells.

So don't pass by the market store or the fruit and vegetable counters in the supermarket. Pick up some of your favourites, grab the juicer and the blender and get going!

A-Z of Fruit

Apples

Apples have been around since the Iron Age and were first cultivated in Egypt. They were so prolific that, in the 1st century AD, Roman Plinus the Elder counted some 36 varieties.

Apples are rich in pectin, a soluble fibre which has been shown in many studies to help reduce cholesterol and regulate blood sugar levels. They also contain boron (a mineral which plays a vital role in the health of our bones and has been found to reduce the pains associated with osteoarthritis); chlorine; copper; iron; magnesium; manganese; phosphorus; potassium; silicon; sodium and sulphur.

Apples are a rich source of vitamin A, which helps to maintain healthy skin, hair and nails and vitamin C. They help to boost our immune system and aid in the fight against cancer due to their antioxidant properties.

The apple season runs from September to November, although many varieties are available all year round. Try to buy apples grown locally as they are the freshest with most of the nutrients still intact. Choose an apple which is firm and has no bruises. Wash them thoroughly to remove the wax coating or try to buy organically grown apples. Never peel your apples, as you will lose the vital pectin, boron and Vitamin A, which are contained in the skin.

Apricots

Apricots are a member of the rose family along with almonds, cherries, peaches and plums. They have been grown for thousands of years and it is said that Alexander the Great brought apricots from their native home in China to Greece in the 4th century BC.

They are a rich source of Vitamin A, beta-carotene, sulphur and salicylates, an anti-inflammatory agent from which aspirin was originally derived. They also contain potassium; phosphorus; calcium; iron and vitamin C. Commercially dried apricots contain sulphur dioxide, a colour preservative, but you should be able to find them without this.

Bananas

Bananas are part of the lily family and have been cultivated since ancient times, originating from east

Asia, although they also thrived in Africa. Antonius Musa, the personal physician of the Roman Emperor Octavius Augustus, promoted the cultivation of bananas brought from Africa from 63–14BC. Bananas are high in potassium, which helps to counterbalance sodium. Studies have shown that consuming one portion of potassium-rich fruit or vegetables can reduce the risk of a stroke by up to 40 per cent.

Bananas are high in magnesium, Vitamin C and tryptophan, an amino acid which makes you sleepy and which is also found in turkey. As a natural antacid, they can help counteract heartburn.

Since bananas ripen at room temperature, buy them when they are still green. You will also find that other fruits in their vicinity ripen faster due to the mixture of ethylene gas and carbon dioxide released by their seeds.

Blackberries

These lovely dark blue fruit can be found across Europe and North America and are an excellent source of vitamin C, potassium, iron, calcium, manganese and bioflavonoids.

A study by Professor Herbert Langford of the University of Mississippi in Jackson in the USA has found that the high content of potassium can reduce high blood pressure and that blackberries are rich in antioxidants, which help to prevent heart diseases.

Readily available in the summer months of July and August, you can also buy blackberries frozen and so enjoy them all year round.

Blueberries

Blueberries are also known as bilberries, whortleberries and hurtleberries, and are a lovely deep blue colour. They are never around for long enough, so when you see them at your supermarket, make a run for them.

In Russian folk medicine, blueberries are used as a preventative measure and cure for flux and other abdominal problems. They have strong antioxidant qualities and studies have shown that they improve night vision and contain a substance which helps in urinary tract and bladder infections just like cranberries. Blueberries contain the ideal combination of Iron and vitamin C, which together enable the body to absorb more iron than it would normally if the vitamin C were not present.

Blueberries are in season from June to August but are also available frozen all year round.

Cantaloupe Melon

Cantaloupe melons are full of antioxidants such as beta-carotene and vitamin C and contain high amounts of vitamin A and potassium, which reduces the risk of stroke and ensures that our muscles relax and contract properly.

They are available in the summer months and a study has shown that when purchased during the peak season they contain higher levels of niacin, riboflavin, thiamine, ascorbic acid, folacin and chromium than at any other time.

Cherries

The cultivation of cherries dates back to 300BC which makes them one of the world's oldest cultivated fruit. Part of the rose family, they are a rich source of vitamins A and C as well as calcium, iron, magnesium and potassium.

Cherries nourish the skin and nerves, and are believed to be a good cleanser of the kidneys and livers by flushing out toxins from the body. Available in different sizes and colours, ranging from large black to yellow-red to smaller red, they can be frozen, but it is best to remove the pips before doing so.

Cranberries

Found in North America and Canada, cranberries were used by Native Americans as a preservative due to their high content of benzoic acid. Studies have shown that cranberry juice helps to prevent urinary tract and bladder infections, as it prevents bacteria from sticking to the walls of the urinary tract. They are a good source of vitamin C, which enhances the immune system, and help in calcium absorption.

Available in the autumn months, they can easily be frozen and enjoyed all year round.

Dates

These fruit have been around for thousands of years and were eaten when travelling across the deserts, as they are rich in carbohydrates. Dates also contain calcium, iron, magnesium, potassium and fibre.

They are very sweet in flavour, so when adding them to juices be careful how many you use. People suffering from diabetes and hypoglycaemia should avoid them as well as figs. You can buy dried dates all year round and you only need to remove the pits before using them.

Figs

Mentioned in the Bible, figs are a good source of carbohydrates, calcium, iron, magnesium and potassium and have been used for medicinal purposes as a diuretic and laxative.

The season for fresh figs is mid June to mid October, and they should be used quickly since they only last a few days. However, you can freeze them either sliced or peeled. Dried figs are higher in minerals but also calories than fresh ones. As with dates, they are very sweet and should be used sparingly.

Grapefruit

Believed to originate from Jamaica, grapefruits come in three flesh colours – yellow, pinkish or red flesh – and are a very good source of vitamin C, being a member of the citrus family. They contain pectin, which can help reduce cholesterol levels, and potassium which helps to counterbalance sodium. The antioxidants found in grapefruit help to fight against cancer and pink grapefruit in particular are a great source of beta-carotene.

Grapes

Cultivated for 5000 years, details of grapevines can be found in ancient Egyptian writings.

Grapes are a good source of vitamin C and potassium, but also contain thiamine, which is part of the vitamin B family and helps the nervous and immune system along with vitamin B6. Grapes come in two colours, green and red, and when grapes are ripe, they are full of natural sugar. The more yellow the green grape, the more sugar it contains. Red grapes should have a rich, dark colour. If you are using a juicer, don't worry about the pips, but try to buy seedless grapes if using them in a blender.

Guava

These fruit come from a tree and may well have been first cultivated in Peru before spreading to Mexico.

Very high in vitamin C (higher in fact than citrus fruits), guava also contain vitamin A, which helps maintain healthy skin, and vitamin B6, which is needed to make haemoglobin. The fruit also has antiseptic properties and is used for treating stomach upsets, diarrhoea and skin disorders.

Guava should be a greenish-yellow in flavour and the seeds, which are high in pectin and help reduce cholesterol levels, can be used in your drinks.

Kiwi

Native to eastern Asia, the people of New Zealand were the first to recognize their great value. Kiwis are high in vitamin C, making them good immune system boosters, and potassium, which reduces the risk of strokes. They also contain beta-carotene and niacin. High in dietary fibre, kiwi can help to regulate blood sugar levels.

They can taste quite sharp because the taste comes from the seeds.

Lemons

Used for hundreds of years in many different cultures, the Romans believed that the lemon would protect them against death resulting from poisonous snakebites. Lemons are high in vitamin C, which through its antioxidant properties helps to fight against cancer.

The acid taste of lemons can bring out the flavour of many other fruits and vegetables, so they are great for any juice recipe that lacks that little bit of zest.

Limes

Cultivated for thousands of years in parts of South America, limes were used between 1795 and 1815 by British sailors to help prevent the dreaded scurvy, and it was this consumption which gave rise

Nectarines

A cousin of the peach and thought to be named from the word 'nektar', the heavenly juice of the nectarine was supposed to be enjoyed by the Greek gods.

They are a good source of vitamin C and contain beta-carotene, which keeps our bones strong.

The nectarine's skin is smoother than that of a peach, and it is sweeter with a slightly higher nutritional value than peaches.

to the British being nicknamed 'limeys'.

Limes are high in vitamin C, but have a less acidic taste to them than lemons. They are smaller than lemons and have a green skin and flesh.

Mangoes

Grown in India for thousands of years and available in many varieties ranging in colour from green to yellow, and red, with purple or orange shading, mangoes are high in vitamins A and C. Their high beta-carotene content makes them a great immune system booster and may prevent cancers of the stomach, colon, bladder, mouth and breast, while the vitamin E content in mangoes is good for muscles, red blood cells, eyes and skin. They also have great antioxidant properties, which help to prevent cancer.

Mangoes can be left to ripen at room temperature. Their rich creamy texture and delicious taste makes them the perfect fruit to use on their own or blended together with other fruits.

Oranges

Natives of south-east Asia, Columbus brought oranges back to Europe from his travels.

They are a good source of vitamin C and also contain calcium, important for bones and teeth, and potassium. The inner part of the orange's skin contains pectin, and the fruit is also an excellent source of folate, which is a B vitamin and important for pregnant women, because it is responsible for the production and maintenance of new cells.

Papaya

Native to Central America, the papaya is very high in vitamins A and C and contains some calcium, iron, phosphorus and potassium, plus an enzyme called papain, a protein digestant. Papaya juice is an energy booster due to its natural sugars, a cleanser of the kidneys, liver and intestines and a good appetite stimulant.

Ripe papayas have a yellow-gold colour, and a creamy rich texture with a subtle sweet taste.

Passion fruit

Passion fruit come from the Amazon region. The ripe fruit is brown in colour and slightly wrinkled with a sweet juicy flavour. Passion fruit are a rich source of vitamins B3 and C and beta-carotene. A good source of the essential bone-building minerals calcium and magnesium, they also contain phosphorus, potassium, sodium and sulphur. The brown-black seeds can be removed from the flesh before juicing them, but if you don't mind a bit of crunchiness in your juice, peel the fruit and scoop the flesh out with the seeds.

Pawpaw

Native Americans used to enjoy them as a very nutritious and delicious fruit. The rich, creamy texture of pawpaw makes them a good substitute for bananas in any recipe. Pawpaws are high in vitamin C, copper, iron, magnesium and manganese and are a good source of potassium, some B vitamins, calcium, phosphorus and zinc. The vitamin C content in pawpaws is three times higher than that in apples, twice as much as in bananas and one third as much as in oranges, and they also exceed apples in their content of essential amino acids.

Available from August to October, you should find them in your local markets or supermarkets.

Peaches

These lovely, sweet fruit originated in China but were brought by the Spanish to Europe and North America. The peach is a member of the rose family, and therefore a cousin of apricots, almonds, cherries and plums.

Peaches are rich in vitamins A, B1, which responsible for processing protein, fats and carbohydrates, B2 and C. You will also find minerals such as calcium, iron and potassium. Peach juice cleanses the intestine and is known to prevent morning sickness in pregnant women.

Available in summer, the skin of a peach is slightly downy.

Pear

A kin to apples, pears have been cultivated since 2000 BC and were brought to Europe via central Asia.

Pear juice contains vitamins A, B and C, folic acid and calcium, and pears are a good source of dietary fibre. The folic acid is important for pregnant women for the normal growth and development of

their babies, while calcium prevents cramps and is necessary for healthy muscles and nerves.

Pears have a rich texture and creamy flavour. Never peel them as you loose all the vital vitamin C and pectin, which is contained in the skin. Fresh pears are available during the autumn, but some varieties are imported all year round.

Pineapples

Originating from South America, pineapples were also brought to Europe by Christopher Columbus. They are very high in vitamin C and potassium and contain an enzyme called bromelin, which is very beneficial to the body. It helps in the treatment of angina, arthritis, bronchitis, burns, and menstrual and digestive problems to name but a few. Pineapples also help to soothe sore throats.

When you can easily remove a leaf from its stalk, you know you have a ripe pineapple. Their creamy rich texture and sweet-acidic flavour make you feel instantly as if you were on holiday, and pineapple juice mixes well with many fruits.

Plums

These luscious fruit have a long history, and are mentioned in early writings by Confucius dating back to 479 BC. Pompey the Great introduced plums into the orchards of Rome, and they are a sign of wisdom and great age in Chinese mythology.

A good source of vitamins A and C, potassium and fibre, they are available from May to late October and will soften at room temperature, if not fully ripened. Dried plums are called prunes and are known for their vitamin A content and both prunes and plums are known for their laxative effect.

Pomegranate

Initially believed to be from China, the pomegranate actually comes from Persia. Pomegranates, with their delicious red seeds, are full of vitamin C, which helps to regulate cholesterol levels, and potassium, which helps to counterbalance sodium. Readily available during the autumn months in all good supermarkets, they are also used as a mouth gargle in parts of Iran and Iraq.

Raspberries

Sadly, fresh raspberries have all too short a season, being at their best only around the month of June. However, you can buy them frozen, if you like. They are very sweet in flavour and have been known to

help against the common cold or flu since they are full of vitamin C to help boost the body's immune system. Raspberries also contain potassium and folic acid which is important for pregnant women.

Sharon fruit

This fruit is widely known in the Middle East, but has been grown in China for thousands of years. Its name comes from the Sharon region near Tel Aviv in Israel where it is grown, but it is also known as kaki fruit or persimmon. Sweet tasting and tomato-shaped, with a shiny peel and the colour of an orange, research carried out suggests that the Sharon fruit contains a higher amount of dietary fibre, minerals and polyphenols, which are antioxidants, than apples. Sharon fruit are also an excellent source of vitamin C and are in season during the autumn and winter.

Strawberries

Grown originally in North America and used in many dishes by native Americans, strawberries are very low in calories and high in vitamin C, and have been used to treat skin and gum problems, and fever. They are a good source of potassium, which helps to restore normal function to the kidneys, as well as folic acid, which helps to maintain healthy DNA.

Strawberries contain a natural painkiller in the form of salicylates, a plant substance similar to aspirin, and a vital component called ellagic acid, which is also found in grapes and cherries. Research has shown that ellagic acid prevents carcinogens from turning healthy cells into cancerous ones.

The strawberry season is really from May to late July, although it is possible to buy imported varieties at other times of the year.

Tomato

The tomato is a fruit and not, as commonly believed, a vegetable. It originates from South America and was brought to Europe by Spanish explorers.

Full of antioxidants which help to prevent many forms of cancer, tomatoes also contain beta-carotene, necessary for healthy eyes and the formation of bones, vitamin C, and the minerals calcium and magnesium. Tomato juice has been found to be good for cleansing and kick-starting the liver and kidneys.

Watermelon

Watermelons come from Africa where, as one might imagine, they are a good source of water supply in the desert. Mark Twain wrote that when one has tasted watermelon one 'knows what angels eat'.

Consisting of 90 per cent water and low in calories, watermelon is a rich source of the vitamins A and C and magnesium and potassium. It is also very good for cleansing the kidneys and bladder and has a mild diuretic action, which helps to flush out excess fluids from the body.

The watermelon season is from May to September. The best way to select a good ripe watermelon is to flick your thumb against it and the melon should produce a deep rich sound.

A-Z of Vegetables

Alfalfa

A sprouting bean just like bean sprouts, alfalfa can be grown at home very easily and is at its highest nutritional value when the green shoots start to appear. It is then that the vitamin C content should have multiplied by as much as 600 times. Alfalfa is also very rich in vitamins A, K and P and contains good amounts of copper, chromium, calcium, iron, iodine, magnesium, manganese, potassium, phosphorus and zinc.

Alfalfa juice has been classified by many as one of the healthiest because of its high content of vitamins and minerals and has been used for a variety of conditions. It is very strong in flavour and is best consumed mixed with other vegetables or fruits.

You can find alfalfa sprouts in all good health shops.

Asparagus

Cultivated for a long time in Europe and Asia, asparagus is a good source of vitamins A and C, as well as calcium, potassium, some sodium and iron.

It has a cleansing effect on the kidneys, helping to flush out excess fluids along with toxins which make it helpful for conditions of acne and general skin disorders, which are the usual signs of an overloaded system or poor diet. Asparagus is also mild on the digestive system and can prevent constipation.

Asparagus is in season in the spring and summer, but you can also buy it in jars from your local supermarket.

Avocado

The avocado comes from South America, but is now extensively grown in California. Avocados are a rich source of vitamins B6 and C. Vitamin B6 plays an important role in the production of hormones and neurotransmitters, and helps to convert energy from carbohydrates. High in monounsaturated fats (the good kind!) and folate, avocados should still be consumed in moderation.

Avocados are great for your skin and have been used to combat dry skin and scalp problems. They are in season during the winter and spring and will ripen once they have been picked from the tree. They should be soft with no blemishes on their skin.

Bean sprout

The bean family is the most widely available in the world and has many varieties. Sprouting beans will remove their gas-producing qualities but, more importantly, the vitamin content also soars dramatically. Bean sprouts are rich in vitamin C and iron, which together enable the body to absorb more iron than would normally be possible if there were no vitamin C present. So they are helpful for conditions such as broken bones, fatigue, fluid retention and cancer. The juice has a strong, fresh flavour and mixes well with other vegetable juices. Bean sprouts are widely available in supermarkets.

Beetroot

Beetroot juice has been used as a blood-builder and body cleanser in traditional medicine. The fresh raw juice is a powerful cleanser of the liver and a good tonic for the digestive system in general. Beetroot contains vitamins A, B6 and C and the minerals calcium, chlorophyll, iron, magnesium and potassium.

When using beetroot, be careful not to use too much because the strong cleansing properties can make you feel nauseous. Beetroot is sweet in flavour and combines well with other vegetables or fruits.

Fresh beetroot can be purchased throughout the spring and summer months.

Broccoli

Broccoli is one of the family of cruciferous vegetables, which are known for their protective powers against cancer. Other members include cabbage, cauliflower, Brussels sprouts, kale, radishes, horseradish and turnips. The cruciferous family contains chemical compounds called indoles and carotenids, which have been identified as being responsible for their protective powers. These are plant pigments. Indole is a volatile oil and stimulates the circulation. Carotenoids are yellow or red pigments found in plants and animals and are related to vitamin A. The most widely known is beta-carotene, which has been shown in many studies to inhibit the activation of cancer cells. Broccoli contains powerful antioxidants and is a good source of iron. Broccoli can be found in the supermarkets throughout the year but it is really in season in spring and autumn.

Cabbage

Another member of the cruciferous family and also high in vitamin C, cabbage has long been known for its healing powers and traditional medicine has used

it for a number of ailments, such as constipation, bronchitis, asthma and bladder disorders. The pigment chlorophyll found in cabbage is almost identical to the haemoglobin in our blood and along with iron it makes it a good tonic for anaemia. Consuming raw cabbage juice can cause gas or cramps, so it is best diluted with other juices or water. It has a distinct but pleasant flavour and mixes well with apple and carrot.

You can find it all year round, which makes it a good vegetable to have on your list to use in juices.

Capsicums (see Peppers)

Carrots

Who has not yet heard of the healing powers of carrots? They are teeming with antioxidants, such as vitamins A, C and E, and are so rich in beta-carotene that one carrot can set you up for the day ahead. They have been widely acknowledged as helping to fight various cancers and have been found to be good for respiratory infections, and disorders of the eyes and skin.

Carrots are a good source of folic acid and carrot juice has a cleansing affect on the liver and is a great rejuvenator of the skin. If you ever think that you are turning orange from drinking too much carrot juice, just be sure to reduce the amount of juice you consume ever so slightly and the problem will go away. Better still, dilute the carrot juice with other juices. Thanks to its sweet flavour, carrot juice is a perfect ingredient to any recipe.

Celery

Hippocrates believed celery helped to calm nerves. Maybe because it is rich in calcium. It also has a strong effect on the kidneys, helping to eliminate waste via the urine, and is useful for constipation and fluid retention. King Henry VIII was given celery juice to help heal his rashes caused by overconsumption of rich food and wines.

Celery is not only high in vitamin A but also contains some vitamin C and B. A good source of potassium and magnesium, celery is readily available during autumn and winter. Mix it with other vegetables, or some fruits, as it has a strong, bitter flavour, which is not necessarily to everyone's taste.

Cucumbers

Everyone likes cucumbers, they are so refreshing, versatile, low in calories and good for your hair, skin and nails. Their cooling properties make them a good food for fevers, but they also have diuretic properties and help with fluid retention and weight loss.

Cucumber contains calcium, potassium and silicon, a mineral necessary for building connective tissue, which holds our bones, muscles, tendons and ligaments in place.

Cucumbers are found throughout the year: just ensure that the cucumber feels firm with no soft spots.

Fennel

Fennel has been around for centuries and was used a lot by the Romans. It is thought to relieve the symptoms of acid indigestion due to its rich alkaline mineral content, which is similar to celery, as well as help with respiratory infections, menstrual cramps and relax the nerves. Fennel contains calcium, magnesium, potassium and phosphorus and some vitamins A and B-complex. The most commonly used type of fennel is called Florence fennel and has a sweet aniseed flavour. Do not drink it undiluted, unless you like the strong aniseed flavour. Mix it with other vegetables or fruits which will hide the flavour but still give the relief you seek. Fennel is in season during the autumn.

Garlic

Used for many centuries, the healing powers of garlic have been widely acknowledged. Much research has been undertaken to show the benefits garlic has on a wide range of ailments. Garlic breath can make you a social outcast, but it has very strong cleansing properties and is good for the entire system; from stimulating the appetite to dissolving mucus in the sinus cavities, lungs and bronchial tubes. Furthermore, garlic has antibacterial, antifungal and antiviral abilities.

Available all year round, choose a bulb which is hard when pressed.

Ginger

Widely used in cooking in Eastern countries and known more in the West as an ingredient in biscuits, ginger is also known as a digestive tonic and as a help in preventing morning sickness, as well as nausea and motion sickness. Often used in drinks to help combat colds and blocked noses, ginger is stimulating to the liver because it helps to remove toxins from the system.

You can find fresh ginger root in most supermarkets, or local markets, and it is a very cheap but important ingredient.

Kale

Another member of the cruciferous family, Kale is a good source of bone-building calcium and blood-building iron. It also contains phosphorus and potassium, and is a very good source of vitamin A.

Kale contains chlorophyll, which is the green pigment found in plant food and which has antioxidant and anticancer properties. Due to its cleansing action, it improves the circulation and respiration of cells helping with eye and skin disorders, asthma, arthritis and hay fever.

In season during autumn and winter, its strong, bitter flavour will not be to everyone's taste despite being good for you, so mix it with other green vegetables.

Lettuce

Lettuce has been around for many centuries and is native to Asia. There are now many different varieties of lettuce on the market and it is full of goodness, great in taste and low in calories. Romaine lettuce has been found consistently to contain higher amounts of calcium, magnesium, iron, phosphorus, potassium, sodium, zinc, and vitamins A, B3 and C than iceberg lettuce, while the darker-leafed lettuces have a greater concentration of vital phytochemicals.

During World War II, lettuce was used as a sedative, but it also helps with constipation, promotes hair growth, calms the nerves and relaxes the muscles.

Lettuce can now be found all year round. It has a strong, slightly bitter flavour, but mixes well with other vegetables or fruits.

Parsley

Used in many parts of the world as a general tonic with particular benefits to the digestive system and kidneys, parsley has been said to relieve menstrual pains, while the leaves are often put on bruises, sprains and insect bites. It is also meant to freshen garlic breath.

Parsley is rich in chlorophyll, an antioxidant and cancer preventative, as well as being a good source of vitamins A and C. The potassium in parsley is meant to be good for most skin disorders as it has an alkalising effect on acidic blood.

Parsley can be grown at home from seed or bought as a ready-grown plant. Strong in flavour, it is better to blend it with other juices.

Parsnip

Similar to carrots in shape and texture, but creamy coloured, parsnips are a good source of vitamin C, chlorine, phosphorus, potassium and silicon, making them important for good skin, hair and nails.

Parsnip is an autumn vegetable and will store well in a cold environment, such as a shed or refrigerator. It is best used mixed with other vegetables as it has a strong flavour.

Peppers (Capsicums)

Although part of the nightshade (belladonna) family, peppers are a popular food that we all love. They come in three colours: green, red and yellow, the latter two being full of beta-carotene. A good source of iron, potassium and silicon and with a very high content of vitamin C, peppers make the ideal food for skin, hair and nails. The red and yellow peppers contain four times as much vitamin C as oranges, and 100g (4 oz) of green pepper will give 1000mg of vitamin C.

The pepper's seasons are summer and autumn and, with its sweet taste, it makes a wonderful addition to to any fruit or green juice.

Radish

Radishes come in many shapes, but the most widely known is probably the little red globe-shaped variety. The radish is part of the cruciferous family (see Broccoli and Cabbage) with their attendant properties. More traditionally, however, radishes are recommended for problems of the liver and gall bladder, as they stimulate the discharge of bile. They have also been used by German doctors to treat constipation.

When eating a radish you instantly feel your nose clearing, so it is beneficial when treating sinus problems. But radish juice is soothing and cleansing to the whole body and is also used for lung and skin disorders and asthma.

Radishes can now be found all year around in supermarkets.

Spinach

As children, most of us probably did not like spinach, but we all knew that it gave Popeye his muscles and strength. Spinach is a native of Asia and its dark green leaves make it an excellent source of chlorophyll. High in beta-carotene and other carotenoids, spinach is one of the best plants to fight off cancer, better even than carrots. Other nutrients found in spinach are the vitamins A and B complex, as well as calcium, iron, magnesium, phosphorus, potassium and sodium. And its high alkaline mineral content makes spinach very good for gums and teeth.

Spinach also contains oxalic acid which is metabolised through exercise.

Autumn and winter are the seasons for spinach. Strong in flavour, it is best used in combination with other juices.

Watercress

Do not underestimate the power of watercress, as it is part of the cruciferous family and should be high on anyone's agenda as a cancer-preventative food. It is very rich in sulphur and, together with chlorine and phosphorus, also acid forming. A powerful cleanser and normaliser of the body, watercress is especially beneficial against infections of the digestive, respiratory and urinary system. Always mix watercress with other juices.

Fruit and Vegetable Chart

Spring	Summer	Autumn	Winter
Avocados	Apricots	Apples (locally grown)	Avocados
Bananas	Asparagus	Bananas	Bananas
Basil	Bananas	Beetroot	Broccoli
Broccoli	Basil	Broccoli	Carrots
Carrots	Blueberries	Cabbage	Cabbage
Cucumbers	Carrots	Carrots	Celery
Lettuce	Cherries	Celery	Chinese cabbage
Peppers	Cucumbers	Chinese cabbage	Cucumber
Radishes	Grapes	Cranberries	Fennel
Spinach	Lemons	Cucumbers	Grapefruit
	Lettuce	Dates	Kiwi
	Mangoes	Fennel	Oranges
	Melons	Figs	Nuts
	Nectarines	Grapefruit	Pears
	Peaches	Grapes	Radish
	Peppers	Lettuce	Spinach
	Strawberries	Lemons	
	Tomatoes	Limes	
	Watermelon	Kale	
		Kiwi	
		Mangoes	
		Nuts	
		Papaya	
		Parsnip	
		Passion fruit	
		Pawpaw	
		Pears	
		Peppers	
		Pineapple	
		Plums	
		Pomegranates	
		Sharon fruit	
		Spinach	

Herbs

Herbs are a wonderful ingredient to many traditional dishes and I have used some from the list below in the recipes to add that extra bit of aroma. Not only do they give a drink a great extra flavour, but also they have been found to possess many healing properties. The list below is by no means exhaustive but it will give you some ideas as to the benefits of these herbs.

If you would like to know more about the healing properties of herbs, I recommend that you do some extra reading (there are some great specialist herb books around), or perhaps consult a herbalist.

Anise or Star Anise	Has a strong sweet flavour and is used in the East to cure flatulence. It can be used together with other herbs in tea. Apparently, it may prevent some cancers.
Basil	Widely known as the main ingredient of pesto sauce, you can grow basil easily in a window box which gives you an all-year-round supply of this delicious herb. Basil has calming properties and is a natural tranquillizer – great if you suffer from insomnia. Basil is also meant to be very good for the heart as well as for people suffering from arthritis.
Black Pepper	A stimulant to the digestive system, pepper also clears your sinuses and can relieve constipation and flatulence.
Cinnamon	We all love the taste of cinnamon; it's a great addition to many dishes. Cinnamon is a good tonic for indigestion and flatulence and with its warming properties helps the whole system combat flu and other viral infections. But did you know that cinnamon has potent antiseptic properties too?
Cloves	Cloves, like cinnamon, are known for their antiseptic properties. A great aid for toothache and as an additive in tea, it enhances the flavour beautifully. It has also been used for diabetes.

Coriander	Has a strong flavour and is usually added to many meat dishes. Coriander is good for indigestion, colicky pain and flatulence. A good all rounder, which is meant to help the body easily flush out toxins, it is also used as an aphrodisiac.
Cumin	Delicious in flavour and added to many dishes in Middle Eastern cuisine, cumin is meant to be good for flatulence and curing colic.
Lemon Balm	Grows everywhere and has a strong smell and flavour. I never knew how good it really is for us – helpful for insomnia, digestive disorders, nausea, headaches, and very calming with antispasmodic properties.
Lemongrass	Known as an ingredient in Thai cooking, lemongrass is very strong in flavour which makes it a good ingredient.
Marjoram	Has calming and antispasmodic properties. It is good for flu and cold symptoms as well as headaches and nervous tension. An all-rounder, which you can easily grow in a window box and enjoy.
Mint	There are many varieties of mint around, and it is a popular ingredient in many dishes and drinks. Mint can be very beneficial to the digestion, with antispasmodic and anti-inflammatory properties. In the Middle East, mint is consumed in tea, which is absolutely delicious and believed to be an aphrodisiac.
Nasturtium	This plant is so easily grown at home with its brightly coloured flowers and is so good for you, as it contains the vitamins A, B3, C and E, plus the minerals iron, sulphur and essential fatty acids. It has a peppery flavour and you can find it in good health shops as seeds or drops. Nasturtium is meant to be beneficial for chronic bronchitis and catarrh
Nutmeg	Another versatile herb, which in small doses is good for our digestion, but if used in large quantities can be hallucinogenic.

Oregano	This always reminds me of pizza. A very versatile herb used much in the Mediterranean kitchen, oregano aids digestion and is good for the respiratory system due to being an effective antiseptic.
Rosemary	A wonderful herb, again used in Mediterranean cuisine, rosemary is beneficial to the digestion, especially for the digestion of fat, with antiseptic and antispasmodic properties. It helps combat painful periods, mental fatigue and poor circulation. Rosemary is meant to be an anti-rheumatic and cardiovascular tonic, so it is good for arthritis and heart conditions.
Sage	Comes in many varieties and colours but can be grown easily at home. A great friend to the digestive system, sage also stimulates and calms the nervous system. It is good for people suffering from stress or nervous exhaustion, and has antiseptic, anti-fungal and astringent properties.
Tea – Black	A powerful stimulant to the body
Tea – Green	Used mainly in Asia, green tea is meant to help in keeping the metabolism high which is maybe why in those parts of the world it is drunk after meals.
Thyme	A powerful antiseptic and a general stimulant to the body, thyme is used as a gargle against coughs and colds. It also gives many meat dishes their beautiful flavour.

The Things You Don't See

Sometimes it's difficult to understand why eating fruit and vegetables is good for you. After all, if you simply think of food as fuel for the body, what's wrong with a burger and fries? Answer: nothing. It fills you up and keeps you going. But there is more to fruit and veg than meets the eye. Anyone who keeps up to date with developments in make-up, and especially skincare, will be well aware of the way words like "antioxidant" and "free radicals" have been tossed around when cosmetic companies do their best to explain why the latest expensive cream is the answer to all our prayers. Well, it's easy to toss those words around too when talking about the benefits of eating fresh fruit and vegetables, so in order to set a few things straight, below are some basic explanations of the good things you don't see when you drink one of your favourite health juices or smoothies, plus tables showing the properties of vitamins and minerals.

Antioxidants

Antioxidants are compounds, which can give molecules a negative charge if they need one to protect themselves against free radicals. Free radicals are produced in our body during oxidation (oxygen being a highly volatile substance, which can become unstable and hence "oxidize" a neighbouring molecule). But our bodies generate antioxidant reserves from the food we eat and, through the metabolism of food, can also generate free radicals. When the balance of free radicals overcomes antioxidant resources, abnormalities through cell damage occur in the body which may lead to many of today's illnesses, such as premature aging, heart diseases and some cancers. Free radical cell damage is further increased by smoking, pollution and stress. The vitamins C, E and carotenoids, which include beta-carotene, lupein and lycopene, and the minerals selenium and zinc have been all identified as antioxidants. They strengthen the immune system and help the body fight infections.

Excellent sources of carotenoids include red, orange, yellow and some dark green leafy vegetables and fruit; vitamin C is found in fruit and vegetables and vitamin E is obtained from nuts, cereals, seeds and whole grains. Nuts, seeds and seafood are an excellent source of zinc and selenium.

Other non-essential nutrients also contain antioxidant properties and can be found in fresh food. Some of these compounds are anthocyanidins contained in berries and grapes, bioflavonoids found in citrus fruit and tomatoes, onions and garlic and curcumin in mustard, turmeric, yellow pepper and corn.

Phytochemicals

Phyto means plant in Greek. Phytochemicals are simply compounds found in plants. The number of known phytochemicals is growing steadily and more research needs to be conducted to examine their beneficial effects and how we may use them. It is known that they work in conjunction with other nutrients and some have powerful antioxidant properties. Phytochemicals are not essential for the body to function properly like protein, carbohydrates, fat, vitamins and minerals but are involved in biochemical reactions, so promoting wellness and decreasing the risk of many diseases. Those that have been identified include carotenoids which I have already mentioned under antioxidants, but flavonoids are also found in black and green tea, onions, red wine and apples and may help to prevent blood clots and have beneficial effects on cholesterol levels. The cruciferous vegetables such as broccoli, cauliflower, cabbage, brussel sprouts, kohlrabi and watercress contain the phytochemical indoles, which are believed to reduce the risk of breast cancer and isothiocyanates and sulforaphane, which promote the production of anti-cancer enzymes. Saponins are found in whole grains such as wheat and rye and are believed to help fight against cancer and heart diseases.

Vitamins

Vitamins are needed to make all our body processes happen, and perform a variety of tasks in order to help maintain health and promote growth. They do this in conjunction which each other but each vitamin also has its own specific functions. We need them in order to utilize other essential nutrients, such as amino acids, fatty acids, carbohydrates and sugars. There have been many discussions about how much of each vitamin we need. Most animals, with a few exceptions, produce about 3–16,000mg of vitamin C in their body per day, when the Recommended Daily Allowance (RDA) is only 60mg, which is the minimum to prevent scurvy. Over a 15-year period, Dr Emmanuel Cheraskin and colleagues from the University of Alabama studied 13,500 people living in different parts of the USA and found that the healthiest were those eating a diet rich in nutrients and taking supplements. The research also showed that the amount of nutrients taken was 10 or more times higher than the RDA levels and the researchers came up with what they called SONAs (Suggested Optimal Nutrient Allowance for vitamins). In the following table of vitamins the SONA for each has been given.

Vitamins	Function/Benefits	Found in
Vitamin A is a fat-soluble vitamin with strong antioxidant properties and is best absorbed when consumed with protein. The suggested optimal nutrient allowance (SONA) is 2000µg. Retinol is the most usable form of Vitamin A and is found in foods such liver and eggs. Beta-carotene is a provitamin A carotenoid and provitamin A carotenoids, such as the orange pigment found in some plant foods, are converted into Vitamin A.	Helps immune function, antioxidant activity; required for the production of protein, bone and tooth development, growth hormones and reproduction; maintains the skin, hair and intestinal lining; alleviates heavy periods, night blindness, acne, aging process, cervical abnormalities and cataracts	Apricots, asparagus, cantaloupe melon, carrots, mangoes, papaya, peaches, red peppers, spinach, sweet potatoes, dark green vegetables and deep-yellow fruits and vegetables
Beta-carotene Is stored in the tissues and will only be converted to Vitamin A when the body requires it. the SONA is 80–100mg per day.	Powerful antioxidant – slowing down the aging process; useful to boost the immune system, and combat acne, heart diseases; a preventative for some cancers, skin disorders	Red, yellow and orange fruit and vegetables
Vitamin B1 is a water-soluble vitamin, also known as Thiamine. Depending on age, 7.1–9.2mg are the recommended amount	Processes protein, fats and carbohydrates; aids in nerve functions; good for normal appetite and digestion; helps to process alcohol; good for pregnancy and breastfeeding; aids normal growth and development	Brown rice, cantaloupe melons, lentils, oranges, nuts (brazil and pecan), peas, spinach

Vitamins	Function/Benefits	Found in
Vitamin B2 or riboflavin a water-soluble vitamin. The SONA is 2–2.5mg per day	Necessary for processing amino acids and fats in the body; helps in the conversion of carbohydrates to energy; aids normal reproduction, growth, repair of skin, hair, nails and joints; helps skin problems – acne, dermatitis, eczema – rheumatoid arthritis, cataracts, migraines	Almonds, asparagus, broccoli, chicken, halibut, milk, mushrooms, salmon, soybeans, spinach, wheat germ
Vitamin B3 is a water-soluble vitamin, which is not stored in the body, but the body manufactures it from protein. There are two forms of this vitamin: niacin (nicotinic acid) and niacinamide (nicotinamide). Both work in the same way but treat different conditions. The SONA is 25–30mg per day.	Necessary for the release of energy from carbohydrates; aids in the regulation of cholesterol in the body, blood sugar levels; necessary for producing sex and adrenal hormones, pregnancy; combats high cholesterol, diabetes, osteoarthritis, rheumatoid arthritis, migraines	Avocados, cheese, eggs, lentils, liver, meat (lean), milk, pasta, peanuts, poultry, salmon, soybeans, tuna
Vitamin B5 is a water-soluble vitamin and known as Pantothenic acid. It is essential to all forms of life in the form of coenzyme A (CoA). The SONA is 2–7mg.	Essential for energy production and the transportation and processing of fats; combats acne, aging, infections such as colds and flu, migraines, sinusitis, rheumatoid arthritis and osteoarthritis	Avocados, broccoli, chicken, cod, eggs, kidney, lentils, liver, mushrooms, peas, tuna, yeast, yoghurt
Vitamin B6 a water-soluble vitamin. Depending on age and sex, 10–25mg is recommended per day. B6 comes in three major chemical forms and performs a variety of functions in the body, which are all essential for good health.	Needed to make haemoglobin; increases the amount of oxygen carried by haemoglobin; helps to maintain blood sugar levels and the nervous and immune system to function properly; helps to alleviate premenstrual syndrome, carpal tunnel syndrome and asthma	Avocados, bananas, chicken, garbanzo beans, oatmeal, potatoes, spinach, sunflower seeds, trout, tuna, walnuts

Vitamins	Function/Benefits	Found in
Vitamin B12 is a water soluble vitamin, which is stored in the liver in small amounts and bound to the protein in food and released in the stomach during digestion by hydrochloric acid. The SONA is 2–3μg per day.	Aids formation of red blood cells and normal nerve activity, DNA replication; helps prevent anaemia	Beef, chicken, clams, eggs, liver, milk, oysters, pork, salmon, tuna, yoghurt
Folate and folic acid is a water-soluble B Vitamin that occurs naturally in food. The SONA is 800–1000μg per day.	Makes normal red blood cells; helps produce and maintain new cells (important during infancy, e.g. breastfeeding, and pregnancy due to rapid cell division); helps combat alcohol abuse, kidney dialysis, liver disease	Asparagus, avocados, bananas, black-eyed peas, broccoli, lettuce, orange juice, papaya, peanuts, spinach, wheat germ
Vitamin C is the healing vitamin. It is water-soluble and has strong antioxidant properties. It is involved in collagen production, which supports the structure of our body- bones, teeth, ligaments, tendons, cartilage and blood vessels. Animals make their own Vitamin C by synthesising it in the liver from glucose. Depending on age and sex, 400-1000mg are the recommended daily allowance.	Converts food into energy; acts as a natural antihistamine; enhances wound healing; boosts the immune system; helps the nervous system by converting certain amino acids into neurotransmitters; helps fight anaemia, ageing process, asthma, cataracts, colds and flu, eczema, hay fever and heart diseases; recommended for male infertility, cancer, cholesterol	Berries, broccoli, citrus fruits (oranges, grapefruits, tangerines, lemons, limes), strawberries, mangoes, melons, papaya, peppers, potatoes, strawberries, tomatoes, green leafy vegetables

Vitamins	Function/Benefits	Found in
Vitamin D is a fat soluble vitamin The liver and kidney convert vitamin D to its active hormone form. The body manufactures the vitamin after being exposed to sunshine. The SONA is 24μg per day.	Helps maintenance of blood and calcium and phosphorus levels; assists in the absorption of calcium from food; reduces loss of calcium; needed for healthy bones and teeth; may help reduce the risk of some cancers, osteoporosis and Alzheimer's	Mackerels, milk, salmon, sardines
Vitamin E is a fat-soluble vitamin stored in the body rejuvenated by Vitamin C. Vitamin E has strong antioxidant properties which protect cells from free radicals which are by-products of the body's metabolism. The recommended daily allowance is 400-800mg.	Powerful antioxidant; has natural blood thinning properties; may protect against cancer by enhancing immune function; protects Vitamin A levels; helps fight heart disease, cataracts and cervical abnormalities	Broccoli, dandelion greens, eggs, kiwi, liver, mangoes, milk, nuts, seeds, soy, spinach, wheat germ
Vitamin K is a fat-soluble vitamin and is made by the bacteria that line the gastrointestinal tract.	Aids bone formation and blood clotting; helps to transport calcium around the body; alleviates morning sickness, osteoporosis; helps mend fractures	Broccoli, cabbage, cauliflower, cereals, kale, lettuce, soybeans, spinach, green leafy vegetables

Minerals

Minerals, just like vitamins, are vital for good health. They can be found in all types of food as well as water. But, due to over-farming, the mineral content of soil has decreased and this has had a knock-on effect on the amounts found in plants, which is one reason why it's good to buy organic produce. In the table which follows you will find details of all the major minerals we need to keep us going.

Minerals	Function/Benefits	Found in
Calcium is the most common mineral in the body and is vital in the survival of the body.	To maintain healthy bones and teeth, good muscle contraction, transporting neurotransmitters, lowering blood pressure, pregnancy, preventing kidney stones and hypertension	Red beans and white beans, broccoli, kale, milk, spinach, tofu, yoghurt
Chlorine is a gaseous element	Essential for the activation of nerve impulses	Water
Chromium is used to make glucose in the body, and together with insulin controls blood sugar levels	Used in the metabolism and to balance blood sugar levels. Deficiency increases the risk of diabetes and cardiovascular disease, helps to prevent high blood cholesterol	Brewer's yeast, cheese, oysters, potatoes, seafood
Copper is needed for many body functions. the optimum ratio of copper to zinc is 1:10, as excess copper drains zinc levels	Strengthens bones, helps collagen formation, protects eyes against oxidative damage, lowers cholesterol levels, gives relief from pains and joints stiffness	Beans, peas, poultry, dark leafy vegetables
Iodine is non toxic up to 1000 µg per day	Aids function of thyroid gland, converts beta-carotene to Vitamin A, prevents atherosclerosis, protects against breast cancer	Table salt – it is best to use salts with less sodium and a higher content of chloride
Iron is used in the formation of healthy blood	Needed for producing haemoglobin, metabolises B Vitamins, aids immune function	Red meats, green leafy vegetables, such as spinach and kale

Minerals	Function/Benefits	Found in
Magnesium is needed by every cell in the body. Half of the body's magnesium is combined with calcium and phosphorus in bones. Only 1 per cent is found in blood	Helps prevent diabetes, osteoporosis, headaches including migraines, heart disease, PMS, kidney stones and gallstones. NB: Alcohol increases excretion of magnesium in urine	Avocado, broccoli, chocolate, nuts, pumpkin seeds, spinach, soybeans, wheat germ
Manganese is an antioxidant. High intake inhibits absorption of copper, iron and zinc and vice versa	Aids energy production, muscle contraction, bone growth, regulates insulin levels, prevents allergies, cataracts, osteoporosis, memory loss, multiple sclerosis.	Fruits, nuts, vegetables
Molybdenum is an antioxidant. Excess can cause increased production of uric acid.	Helps the body to detoxify sulphite.	Beans, breads, cereals, milk
Phosphorus In its natural free form, phosphorus glows in the dark	In conjunction with calcium maintains bones and teeth, aids kidney function	Dark green vegetables, eggs, fruits, fish, meat, milk, nuts, seeds
Potassium Located within cells and concentrated mainly in muscles but also skin and other tissues. Stress depletes potassium	Helps muscle contraction, nerve function, energy production, regulates water balance and blood pressure, prevents cramps, kidney stones, allergies.	Avocados, bananas, bulgur, dried figs, fish, melons, milk, papaya, potatoes, poultry, sunflower seeds, tomatoes, green leafy vegetables

Minerals	Function/Benefits	Found in
Selenium has antioxidant properties, which help to protect cells from the effects of free radicals.	Helps to fight cancer, cardiovascular disease, arthritis, enhances immune system working together with Vitamin E	Brewer's yeast, brazil nuts, broccoli, cabbage, celery, cucumber, fish, garlic, grains, oatmeal, onions, poultry, radishes
Silicon	Helps formation of blood vessels, connective tissue (along with vitamin C), prevents osteoporosis, good for hair, nails and skin	Skin of fruit and vegetables, husks of cereals
Sodium is made up of a number of compounds, sodium chloride, i.e. table salt, being the most common. Do not take more than 10 per cent of potassium intake.	High salt diet has been associated with a greater risk of high blood pressure, helps to maintain the body's fluid, balance.	Salt – see Iodine
Sulphur	Assists in the production of collagen, good for hair, skin and nails	Beef (lean), dried beans, cabbage, eggs, fish
Zinc is found in almost every body cell and is one of 200 enzymes. It is also a component of insulin	Aids immune system, healing of wounds, normal growth and development during pregnancy, maintains senses of taste and smell, helps fight rheumatoid arthritis, cataracts, cancer	Beef, crab, lamb, oysters, pork, wheat germ

Supplements

Adding a supplement to a drink can help boost any deficiencies in your diet. The following list is by no means complete but gives the reader an insight into some of the more common ones available. Always follow the guidelines on their packages as to usage. *NB: Do not use a supplement without consulting a doctor.*

Acidophilus

Lactobacillus acidophilus is part of the lactobacillus family, so-called "friendly" bacteria. You can buy it usually as tablets or in liquid form. Be sure that the label says the cultures are "live" or active. You will find that they are combined with *Lactobacillus bifidus*.

Algae

When added to any drinks, blue-green algae change the flavour and colour slightly, but they are high in essential vitamins, minerals and amino acids. Available in powder or tablet form.

Aloe

A native to Africa, aloe is a succulent plant. The juice is soothing to the digestion and helps the liver, kidneys and gall bladder to function. You can either keep a plant in your home or buy aloe vera juice.

Bee Pollen

Some call bee pollen nature's perfect food because it strengthens the immune system and provides energy due to its high content of B vitamins. It is also a good source of the vitamins A, C, D, E and minerals. It comes in a variety of forms.

Brewer's Yeast

Often called nutritional yeast, brewer's yeast is found in the wild as a plant but is best known as a by-product of the brewing process. It is full of essential B vitamins and amino acids and is available in tablet, powder or liquid form.

Brahmi

An Indian herb, brahmi is used to improve memory capacity, increase concentration, and relieve insomnia and nervous tension. It is also known to promote fertility and prevent miscarriages. Available in powder or liquid form.

Coenzyme Q-10

Important for building and restoring tissue and cells, Coenzyme Q-10 is produced by the body, but stimulated through exercise. Beneficial when treating heart diseases, high blood pressure and diabetes, it comes in tablet form.

Damiana

Damiana has a reputation as an aphrodisiac and in homeopathic medicine is used to treat female sexual disorders. It has strong anti-depressant properties and you can find it in liquid or dried form.

Echinacea

Echinacea is best known for its immune strengthening properties, stimulating cells responsible for fighting infections and healing wounds. Available in liquid, capsule, tablet or tea form, use echinacea for no longer than 6–8 weeks, as it can lose its power.

Flaxseed Oil

Flaxseed or linseed has been around since ancient times. Its healing properties have been known for centuries. Full of essential fatty acids, flaxseed oil is recognised as being effective in treating conditions from heart disease to cancer. Flaxseed oil needs to be kept in a cool dry place.

Ginkgo Biloba

Studies in the last 30 years showing that ginkgo can benefit the entire body, increasing the flow of blood and oxygen. It may also help in treating eye and ear disorders. Available in liquid, powder and capsule form.

Ginseng

Traditionally used by the elderly to boost mental and physical vitality, ginseng generally helps to strengthen the immune system, reduce blood sugar levels and provide antioxidants. Available in liquid or dried form.

Glucosamine

A natural sugar, glucosamine can be produced naturally and is used to maintain cartilage, the white rubber-like material which cushions the joints. The supplements normally come as glucosamine sulphate tablets or capsules and are sometimes combined with chondroitin sulphate.

Guarana

Guarana comes from the Amazon basin. The seeds of the guarana vine are peeled, dried, roasted and ground to use just like coffee. Even when ground into powder they are not water-soluble so the body cannot absorb guarana quickly, but the caffeine is released into the bloodstream slowly giving energy for hours. Available in powder form and some liquids.

Protein Powder

Protein is necessary for the development, repair and maintenance of body tissues. Adding protein powder to your drinks gives your body energy.

Spirulina

Spirulina is a blue-green algae and its medicinal properties have been known for a long time. It contains the vitamins A, B complex and E, plus eight of the essential amino acids, and various minerals, digestive enzymes and chlorophyll. Although heralded as a miracle cure for arthritis, there is no scientific evidence to support those claims. Available in a variety of forms.

Wheatgrass

Wheatgrass has a high concentration of vital vitamins and minerals. It has a great cleansing effect on the whole body but is better mixed with other juices due to its bitter taste.

Whey

Whey is a protein derived from cow's milk and full of essential amino acids. It is easily absorbed to give a quick boost of energy and usually sold as a powder.

Additives

Additives are very important to the taste of our juices. Some of the recipes would just not be the same without them.

Carob

Carob powder is made from the ground bean of the carob tree, which can be found in the Mediterranean and southern Asia. The dry pod softens on chewing and has a sweet taste to it. It is generally used as a cocoa substitute as it has more vitamins and minerals but fewer fats and calories. You can find carob in all good health shops.

Coconut Milk

Coconut milk is a complete protein extracted from the coconut flesh. A rich source of amino acids, sugars and mineral salts, but high in saturated fat, it should be used in moderation or you can buy reduced fat coconut milk.

Dandelion

Dandelion roots have diuretic properties, helping the body to eliminate uric acid and detoxify the liver. Useful in treating fluid retention, arthritis, rheumatism and PMS bloating and a good tonic for the digestive and urinary system, the leaves are full of potassium, iron and the vitamins A, B, C, and D. Dandelion coffee is made from the roasted dandelion root and is a good tonic for keeping the natural potassium and sodium balance in your body.

Honey

It's sweeter than sugar, so you need less. It is best to buy natural, untreated honey as it contains more minerals than treated honey or sugar.

Milk

Available in various consistencies and with a varying fat content. Milk contains the vitamins B12 and D, which aid the absorption of calcium. phosphorus and potassium from food. Calcium is essential for our bones and teeth. Many people have become intolerant of dairy products and in this book, non-dairy milk products have been used. Infants under 6 months should not consume any cow's milk as their digestive system cannot cope with it.

Nuts

Nuts have been around for millions of years and are a good source of nutrients. High in mono-unsaturated and polyunsaturated fat, which can help to reduce blood cholesterol, they contain the B vitamins that feed our brains and nervous systems as well as vitamin E, a powerful antioxidant. Walnuts, in particular, are a good source of the essential fatty acid Omega-6.

Rice milk

A non-dairy milk made from rice and seeds, rice milk is a very tasty alternative to normal milk and can be used as a substitute for milk in all recipes.

Enriched rice milk contains calcium, vitamins A, B12, D and E, ensuring that you get an adequate supply of these nutrients. Rice milk is low in cholesterol and fat and contains no lactose. You can find it in a variety of flavours in all good health shops and supermarkets.

Seeds

Seeds are a good source of protein, carbohydrates and fat. They contain the antioxidant vitamin E, essential folic acid, vitamin B and the minerals iron, magnesium and zinc. Sunflower, pumpkin, hemp and sesame seeds are a good source of the Omega-6 essential fatty acid. Omega-3 essential fatty acid is found in pumpkin, flaxseed and Hempseed oil. Seeds can help reduce cholesterol and protect against heart diseases.

Soya milk

This comes from soybeans, which are an excellent source of essential vitamins and minerals. Soya milk can be bought in a variety of flavours, sweetened and unsweetened, and it is an excellent alternative to milk, especially for anyone who is intolerant of lactose. Soya milk is suitable for vegetarians, and is gluten free and low in fat and cholesterol.

Sugar

A quick fix for the body to receive energy, sugar is not good for our teeth and will also be stored as fat by the body if it is not used. Unfortunately, processed sugars have most of the vitamins and minerals removed. Fruits contain a natural sugar called fructose and in order for the body to use fructose it needs to convert it into glucose. This in turn slows down the rate of absorption and energy is released gradually.

Tofu

Tofu is another product made from the soybean, and it is a complete protein full of essential amino acids and low in fat. Tofu comes in two forms, firm and soft, or silken, and the latter makes a great ingredient in some of the recipes.

Water

Most of our body consists of water, which is why we are told to drink plenty of it – at least 1.5–2litres (6–10 cups) per day. Water helps to flush out toxins from the body. You can use tap water, or bottled still or sparkling water in the recipes.

Yoghurt

Yoghurt contains the essential vitamins B5 and B12, which are necessary for energy production. Soothing to the digestive tract, yoghurt with "live" cultures is particularly good for maintaining the friendly bacteria in the stomach.

Preparing to juice

Before you start juicing there are a few points which are worthwhile remembering in order to get the most out of your power drinks:

1. Try to buy fruit and vegetables when they are in season, as they will be fresh and most of the nutrients will still be intact.

2. Buy fruit and vegetables grown locally as the less time a food has been transported and stored the more nutrients it still contains.

3. Buy organic.

4. Only buy as much as you need; the longer you store a fruit or vegetable in your home, the more nutrients are lost.

5. Freeze fruits wherever possible so that you have an all year round supply of your favourites.

6. Dilute drinks before giving them to children as they can be too strong and potent for their digestive system. You can do this by adding still or sparkling water, soda, or lemonade. If you prefer your drinks diluted, so be it.

7. Be open minded when juicing, as sometimes the texture and colour can be very different from any juices you may buy commercially.

8. Peel fruit and vegetables with thick skins such as bananas, avocados and mangoes and remove the stones or seeds, e.g. from cherries, avocados, mangoes and papayas.

9. Cut the fruit and vegetables into smaller pieces so that they will fit into your juicer or blender.

10. Always thoroughly wash your fruit and vegetables before use and always use clean equipment.

Feeling and Looking Beautiful

The condition of our skin, our hair, our nails and even our eyes is always a true reflection of how healthy we are, and to achieve a great complexion, shiny hair, strong nails and bright eyes we need to make sure we get a good and varied supply of vitamins and minerals.

Our skin tells us what is going on in our bodies – blemishes, for example, are signs that our bodies are overworked and that we have accumulated toxins which aren't being released via the urinary system, while eczema can be caused by a combination of poor diet and stress and dandruff indicates that the sebaceous glands on the top of the head are either over- or underproducing sebum.

Nails, of course, are a very good indicator of any shortcomings in our bodies. If you have ever had a problem with little white spots appearing on your nails, then it means that you are suffering from a deficiency of zinc and brittle, flaky nails have been known to be caused by a lack of iron.

Dull eyes are another giveaway, as is bad breath, which doesn't help with your social life either!

A balanced intake of the vitamins A, C and E plus the minerals zinc, sulphur, silicon, potassium and copper ensure that you are helping your body in the best way possible. All the drinks in this section are aimed at providing the right dosages of these vitamins and minerals and, if needed, helping to build up those levels that are low.

Tomato Punch

A tonic full of beta-carotene and Vitamins A, B complex, C and E, this will really put the sparkle back in your eyes.

2 tomatoes

3 medium-sized carrots, topped and tailed

1 red pepper, stalk removed and deseeded

1 teaspoon of lemon juice

75g (3oz) tofu

some basil leaves

20 ginkgo biloba drops

Put the carrots, pepper and tomatoes through the juicer. Then transfer the extracted juice into a blender, add the remaining ingredients and blend until smooth. Makes approximately 450ml (2 cups) of juice. Note that the drink will separate after 10–15 minutes.

Energy (kcal): 182 Protein: 9.3g Fat: 4.7g
Saturated fat: 0.5g Monounsaturated fat: 0.1g
Polyunsaturated fat: 0.9g Carbohydrates: 26.9g
Total Sugars: 25.2g Dietary fibre: 8.8g Sodium:
53mg Potassium: 909mg Calcium: 440mg
Magnesium: Iron: 2.62mg Copper: 1.33mg Zinc:
1.0mg Selenium: 1.3µg Vitamin A: 3054µg Beta-
carotene: 18,325µg Vitamin B3: 4.24mg Vitamin
B6: 1.07mg Vitamin B12: 0µg Folic Acid: 70µg
Vitamin C: 312mg Vitamin E: 3.86mg.

Tomato Punch

Thai Kick

A wonderful tasting drink that always reminds me of sunny beaches, the vitamin E contained in the mango is good for muscles, red blood cells, eyes and skin. Mangoes are full of vital beta-carotene and the vitamins A and C. Thai Kick also has a lovely creamy texture.

1 mango, peeled, stoned and diced
juice of ½ lime
150ml (⅔ cup) coconut milk

Place all the ingredients in a blender and mix until smooth. Makes approximately 350ml (just over 1¼ cups) of juice.

> Energy (kcal): 550 Protein: 5.5g Fat: 24.9g
> Saturated fat: 22g Monounsaturated fat: 2g
> Polyunsaturated fat: 0.0g Carbohydrates: 41.4g
> Total Sugars: 40.7g Dietary fibre: 7.0g Sodium: 170mg Potassium: 887mg Calcium: 94mg
> Magnesium: 79mg Phosphorus: 188mg Iron: 3.54mg Copper: 0.36mg Zinc: 0.4mg Selenium: 0µg Vitamin A: 721µg Beta-carotene: 4.32mg
> Vitamin B3: 1.48mg Vitamin B6: 0.38mg Vitamin B12: 0µg Folic Acid: 2µg Vitamin C: 106mg
> Vitamin E: 2.52mg.

The Kid

A wonderful combination of fruits and vegetables make this delicious drink great for improving your skin. The potassium and sodium in the cucumber help to regulate the water balance and flush out the system.

1 mango, peeled, stoned and diced
1 apple, 0cored and diced
½ cucumber, skinned and diced

Put all the ingredients in a blender and mix until smooth. You can add some crushed ice to it if you like. Makes approximately 300ml (1¼ cups) of juice.

> Energy (kcal): 55 Protein: 0.6g Fat: 0.2g
> Saturated fat: 0g Monounsaturated fat: 0g
> Polyunsaturated fat: 0.1g Carbohydrates: 13.6g
> Total Sugars: 13.5g Dietary fibre: 2.5g Sodium: 3mg Potassium: 157mg Calcium: 8mg
> Magnesium: 9mg Phosphorus: 15mg Iron: 0.36mg Copper: 0.06mg Zinc: 0.1mg Selenium: 0µg Vitamin A: 122µg Beta-carotene: 734µg
> Vitamin B3: 0.27mg Vitamin B6: 0.09mg Vitamin B12: 0µg Folic Acid: 1µg Vitamin C: 19mg Vitamin E: 0.82mg.

The Kid

Radiance

This delicious green drink will really help your complexion. The vitamin A and beta-carotene in the ingredients are essential for good skin and the minerals in the cucumber will help get rid of toxins via the kidneys and not the skin.

2 medium-sized carrots, topped and tailed
½ cucumber
½ green pepper
50g (2oz) watercress
150g (6oz) spinach

Feed all the ingredients into a juicer and pour the juices into a glass. Makes approximately 300ml (1¼ cups).

Energy (kcal): 81 Protein: 5.6g Fat: 1.8g
Saturated fat: 0.3g Polyunsaturated fat: 0.2g
Monounsaturated fat: 0.1g Carbohydrates: 11.4g
Total Sugars: 10.6g Dietary fibre: 9.9g Sodium:
235mg Potassium: 1015mg Calcium: 287mg
Magnesium: 94mg Phosphorus: 101mg Iron:
3.85mg Copper: 0.10mg Zinc: 1.2mg Selenium:
2.3ug Vitamin A: 2020ug Beta-carotene:
12,118ug Vitamin B3: 2.07mg Vitamin B6: 0.67mg
Vitamin B12: 0ug Folic Acid: 271ug Vitamin C:
165mg Vitamin E: 3.85mg.

Summer Time

... and the living is easy! So goes the song and the drink matches it. The watermelon has diuretic properties, which help flush the body of toxins, and together with the strawberries it tastes so good.

¼ medium-sized watermelon, skinned and
      diced
150g (6oz) strawberries

Place the ingredients in a blender and mix until smooth. Makes approximately 350ml (just over 1¼ cups) of juice.

Energy (kcal): 102 Protein: 2.2g Fat: 0.8g
Saturated fat: 0.2g Polyunsaturated fat: 0.2g
Monounsaturated fat: 0.2g Carbohydrates: 23.2g
Total Sugars: 23.2g Dietary fibre: 3.6g Sodium:
13mg Potassium: 440mg Calcium: 38mg
Magnesium: 31mg Phosphorus: 54mg Iron:
1.20mg Copper: 0.16mg Zinc: 0.6mg Selenium:
0µg Vitamin A: 79µg Beta-carotene: 472µg
Vitamin B3: 1.10mg Vitamin B6: 0.37mg Vitamin
B12: 0µg Folic Acid: 34µg Vitamin C: 132mg
Vitamin E: 0.50mg.

Summer Time

Silky Too

The ingredients in this drink will really help to cleanse your system and they are good sources of vitamins A and C and beta-carotene to help your skin.

2 medium-sized carrots, topped and tailed
6 leaves of lettuce
1 green pepper, stalk removed and deseeded
50g (2oz) alfalfa

Put all the vegetables through the juicer and pour the juice into a glass. Makes approximately 350ml (just over 1¼ cups) of juice.

> **Energy (kcal): 82 Protein: 4.9g Fat: 1.7g
> Saturated fat: 0.4g Monounsaturated fat: 0.0g
> Polyunsaturated fat: 0.9g Carbohydrates: 13g
> Total Sugars: 12.2g Dietary fibre: 6.9g Sodium:
> 32mg Potassium: 587mg Calcium: 68mg
> Magnesium: 41mg Phosphorus: 108mg Iron:
> 2.01mg Copper: 0.14mg Zinc: 0.9mg Selenium:
> 1.6µg Vitamin A: 1,216µg Beta-carotene: 7,296µg
> Vitamin B3: 1.08mg Vitamin B6: 0.75mg Vitamin
> B12: 0µg Folic Acid: 142µg Vitamin C: 250mg
> Vitamin E: 2.49mg.**

Blood Red

As well as being full of beta-carotene and vitamin C, this beautifully coloured drink also contains silicon, an essential mineral for good skin.

1 apple
1 red pepper, stalk removed and deseeded
1 yellow pepper, stalk removed and deseeded
3 medium-sized carrots, topped and tailed

Put all the ingredients through the juicer and pour into a glass. Makes approximately 400ml (just under 2 cups) of juice.

> **Energy (kcal): 205 Protein: 5.5g Fat: 1.7g
> Saturated fat: 0.3g Monounsaturated fat: 0.0g
> Polyunsaturated fat: 0.9g Carbohydrates: 41.4g
> Total Sugars: 40.7g Dietary fibre: 7.0g Sodium:
> 170mg Potassium: 887mg Calcium: 78mg
> Magnesium: 79mg Phosphorus: 88mg Iron:
> 1.94mg Copper: 0.36mg Zinc: 0.4mg Selenium:
> 0µg Vitamin A: 721µg Beta-carotene: 4.32mg
> Vitamin B3: 1.40mg Vitamin B6: 0.38mg Vitamin
> B12: 0µg Folic Acid: 2µg Vitamin C: 104mg
> Vitamin E: 2.52mg.**

Blood Red

Antioxidant

Asparagus makes the blood more alkaline and helps the body flush out toxins. The vitamins A, C and E will aid the healing of any skin damage.

100g (4oz) asparagus

4 medium-sized carrots, topped and tailed

100g (4oz) radishes

150g (6oz) spinach, thoroughly washed

3 celery sticks

3 cabbage leaves

Feed all the ingredients through the juicer and pour the juice into a glass. Makes approximately 750ml (3¼ cups) of juice.

> **Energy (kcal): 170 Protein: 12g Fat: 3.1g**
> **Saturated fat: 0.6g Monounsaturated fat: 0.2g**
> **Polyunsaturated fat: 1.9g Carbohydrates:24.6g**
> **Total Sugars: 23g Dietary fibre: 19.5g Sodium:**
> **688mg Potassium: 2188mg Calcium: 453mg**
> **Magnesium: 117mg Phosphorus: 256mg Iron:**
> **6.51mg Copper: 0.28mg Zinc: 2.4mg Selenium:**
> **11.4µg Vitamin A: 3,183µg Beta-carotene:**
> **19,101µg Vitamin B3: 4.03mg Vitamin B6: 0.86mg**
> **Vitamin B12: 0µg Folic Acid: 494µg Vitamin C:**
> **148mg Vitamin E: 5.13mg.**

Shiny

For shiny, healthy hair, you will always need a good balance of the right vitamins and minerals and vitamins C and E plus iron, silicon and sulphur have all been identified as essential for healthy hair. Aloe vera is known for its healing properties for the skin, hair and nails and I have added it to this drink as an extra measure.

6 lettuce leaves

150g (60z) spinach, thoroughly washed

3 medium-sized carrots, topped and tailed

3 cabbage leaves

½ bulb of fennel

1 tablespoon of aloe vera juice

Feed all the ingredients (except the aloe vera juice) into the juicer. Add the aloe vera into the glass first before filling it with the juice, stir to mix all the ingredients together. Makes approximately 500ml (2½ cups) of juice.

> **Energy (kcal): 130 Protein: 8.3g Fat: 2.6g**
> **Saturated fat: 0.5g Monounsaturated fat: 0.2g**
> **Polyunsaturated fat: 1.7g Carbohydrates: 19.2g**
> **Total Sugars: 18.3g Dietary fibre: 13.5g Sodium:**
> **253mg Potassium: 1714mg Calcium: 378mg**
> **Magnesium: 104mg Phosphorus: 173mg Iron:**
> **5mg Copper: 0.12mg Zinc: 2mg Selenium:**
> **4.7µg Vitamin A: 2,635µg Beta-carotene:**
> **15,813µg Vitamin B3: 3.47mg Vitamin B6: 0.69mg**
> **Vitamin B12: 0µg Folic Acid: 398µg Vitamin C:**
> **112mg Vitamin E: 3.92mg.**

Antoxidant

Grease Lightning

With the essential vitamins C and E and the minerals iron, silicon and sulphur, this is an excellent drink for boosting the condition of your hair, skin and nails.

3 medium-sized carrots, topped and tailed
½ cucumber
1 green pepper, stalk removed and deseeded
25g (1oz) watercress

Feed all the ingredients into the juicer and then pour into a glass. Makes approximately 300ml (1¼ cups) of juice.

> Energy (kcal): 79 Protein: 3.2g Fat: 1.3g
> Saturated fat: 0.4g Monounsaturated fat: 0.0g
> Polyunsaturated fat: 0.8g Carbohydrates: 14.8g
> Total Sugars: 13.8g Dietary fibre: 7.8g Sodium:
> 53mg Potassium: 517mg Calcium: 98mg
> Magnesium: 28mg Phosphorus: 73mg Iron:
> 1.83mg Copper: 0.07mg Zinc: 0.5mg Selenium:
> 1.2µg Vitamin A: 1,838µg Beta-carotene:
> 11,026µg Vitamin B3: 0.54mg Vitamin B6:
> 0.84mg Vitamin B12: 0µg Folic Acid: 87µg
> Vitamin C: 266mg Vitamin E: 2.71mg.

Pick Me Up

This delicious creamy drink is rich in vitamins A, B, C and E and beta-carotene with all their antioxidant properties. The B vitamins also provide the body with energy. It's a good drink to take to work with you and enjoy as a mid-morning or mid-afternoon snack.

juice of ½ grapefruit
1 kiwi, peeled and diced
juice of 1 orange
½ mango, peeled and diced
75g (3oz) double cream

Place all the ingredients in a blender and mix until smooth. Makes approximately 300ml (1¼ cups).

> Energy (kcal): 442 Protein: 4.3g Fat: 34.2g
> Saturated fat: 21g Monounsaturated fat: 9.7g
> Polyunsaturated fat: 0.1g Carbohydrates: 31.1g
> Total Sugars: 30.8g Dietary fibre: 4.9g Sodium:
> 39mg Potassium: 639mg Calcium: 142mg
> Magnesium: 39mg Phosphorus: 105mg Iron:
> 0.87mg Copper: 0.22mg Zinc: 0.4mg Selenium:
> 2.1µg Vitamin A: 591µg Beta-carotene: 1,024µg
> Vitamin B3: 1.18mg Vitamin B6: 0.34mg Vitamin
> B12: 0.1µg Folic Acid: 68µg Vitamin C: 157mg
> Vitamin E: 1.68mg.

Pick Me Up

Razzleberry

A truly delicious blend of most people's favourite berries, this is loaded with vitamin C to boost the immune system. Cherries are a rich source of the antioxidant vitamins A and C as well as a good source of calcium, iron, magnesium and potassium. They are believed to be a good cleanser of the kidneys and livers because they flush out toxins from the body. It will also give your nails a boost.

100g (4oz) raspberries

100g (4oz) cherries

1 apple, cored and diced

250ml (⅔ cup) cranberry juice

½ teaspoon of vitamin C powder

Put all the ingredients together in a blender and mix until smooth. Makes aapproximately 400ml (just under 2 cups) of juice.

> Energy (kcal): 142 Protein: 3.3g Fat: 0.7g
> Saturated fat: 0.1g Monounsaturated fat: 0.1g
> Polyunsaturated fat: 0.2g Carbohydrates: 33g
> Total Sugars: 33g Dietary fibre: 15.9g Sodium:
> 10mg Potassium: 642mg Calcium: 60mg
> Magnesium: 44mg Phosphorus: 80mg Iron:
> 2.05mg Copper: 0.27mg Zinc: 0.8mg Selenium:
> 1.0µg Vitamin A: 14µg Beta-carotene: 82µg
> Vitamin B3: 0.95mg Vitamin B6: 0.28mg Vitamin
> B12: 0µg Folic Acid: 42µg Vitamin C: 68mg
> Vitamin E: 1.20mg.

All rounder

Parsley is well known as a good breath freshener and the vitamin C and beta-carotene in the carrots and spinach will help fight infections.

3 medium-sized carrots, topped and tailed

150g (6oz) spinach, thoroughly washed

25g (1oz) parsley

Feed all the ingredients into the juicer, starting with the parsley and pour the juice into a glass. Makes approximately 300ml (1¼ cups) of juice.

> Energy (kcal): 90 Protein: 5.8g Fat: 2.0g
> Saturated fat: 0.3g Monounsaturated fat: 0.2g
> Polyunsaturated fat: 1g Carbohydrates: 12.7g
> Total Sugars: 11.8g Dietary fibre: 11.4g Sodium:
> 250mg Potassium: 1,182mg Calcium: 345mg
> Magnesium: 92mg Phosphorus: 105mg Iron:
> 5.82mg Copper: 0.09mg Zinc: 1.4mg Selenium:
> 3µg Vitamin A: 2,709µg Beta-carotene: 16,252µg
> Vitamin B3: 2.34mg Vitamin B6: 0.45mg Vitamin
> B12: 0µg Folic Acid: 290µg Vitamin C: 103mg
> Vitamin E: 3.75mg.

Razzleberry

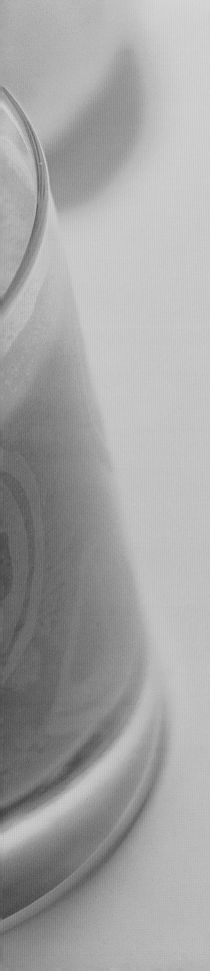

Defuse

The name gives it away, but this is a wonderful drink, which will help rebalance the body's acid-alkaline levels and promote the secretion of toxins via the kidneys.

100g (4oz) asparagus

1 parsnip, topped and tailed

6 cabbage leaves

1 apple, quartered

Put all the ingredients through the juicer, starting with the softest vegetables. Then pour into a glass and drink slowly. Makes approximately 300ml (1¼ cups) of juice.

Energy (kcal): 156 Protein: 8.5g Fat: 1.9g
Saturated fat: 0.4g Monounsaturated fat: 0.3g
Polyunsaturated fat: 1.1g Carbohydrates: 27.5g
Total Sugars: 24.4g Dietary fibre: 13.4g Sodium:
358mg Potassium: 1,096mg Calcium: 164mg
Magnesium: 42mg Phosphorus: 202mg Iron:
2.89mg Copper: 0.23mg Zinc: 1.4mg Selenium:
4.1µg Vitamin A: 206µg Beta-carotene: 1,238µg
Vitamin B3: 2.15mg Vitamin B6: 0.58mg Vitamin
B12: 0µg Folic Acid: 311µg Vitamin C: 143mg
Vitamin E: 2.58mg.

Defuse

Energy Elixirs

Do you ever feel tired at the end of a long day at work, perhaps too tired to go to the gym after the stress of the office? Not surprisingly, there are times when we all need that extra boost to help us through our schedules or to give our bodies the vital nutrients they need to perform a task, such as exercising, and as often happens, it's not easy trying to eat a steady supply of the right things when you're on the go all the time or racing from one meeting to another.

This section contains recipes for some drinks which really are *powerful*, in as much as they will give you that extra boost you need. What's more they taste delicious. If you haven't already tasted it, do also try Tomato Punch (see page 39) which is also packed full of energy-giving properties.

Caramba

You will get a boost of energy from this sweet tasting drink as well as receiving a good dose of the vitamins B, C and E and beta–carotene. It's good to drink either before or after exercise or whenever you need a pick-me-up. If you like, you can also mix it with some yoghurt or soya milk and take it to work with you.

3 medium-sized carrots, topped and tailed

½ pineapple, diced

1 orange, quartered

½ mango

2 teaspoons ginseng powder

Feed the pineapple, orange, mango and carrots into the juicer, but use the carrots last as they are the hardest vegetable and will ensure that all the other juices are extracted. Pour the juice into a glass and stir in the ginseng powder. Makes approximately 300ml (1¼ cups) of juice.

> Energy (kcal): 278 Protein: 4.3g Fat: 1.3g
> Saturated fat: 0.2g Monounsaturated fat: 0.3g
> Polyunsaturated fat: 0.6g Carbohydrates: 66.7g
> Total Sugars: 65.8g Dietary fibre: 12.5g Sodium:
> 46mg Potassium: 1,100mg Calcium: 172mg
> Magnesium: 81mg Phosphorus: 96mg Iron:
> 1.72mg Copper: 0.55mg Zinc: 0.7mg Selenium:
> 2.8µg Vitamin A: 1,880µg Beta-carotene:
> 11,280µg Vitamin B3: 2.24mg Vitamin B6: 0.72mg
> Vitamin B12: 0µg Folic Acid: 80µg Vitamin C:
> 162mg Vitamin E: 2.22mg.

Caramba

Replenish

You cannot get enough of the essential B vitamins for sustained energy and Replenish is an excellent source of those as well as vitamin C, which produces collagen. The calcium in it prevents cramps and is necessary for healthy muscles and nerves, while there is also a lot of good dietary fibre and cholesterol-reducing properties due to the pectin found in pears and oranges.

1 orange, peeled, diced, pips removed

1 pear, cored and diced

½ lemon, peeled, diced, pips removed

75g (3oz) tofu

2 teaspoons ginseng powder

Place all the ingredients in the blender and mix until smooth. Makes approximately 400ml (just under 2 cups) of juice.

> Energy (kcal): 197 Protein: 8g Fat: 3.5g
> Saturated fat: 0.0g Monounsaturated fat: 0.0g
> Polyunsaturated fat: 0.0g Carbohydrates: 35.3g
> Total Sugars: 34.9g Dietary fibre: 3.1g Sodium:
> 17mg Potassium: 623mg Calcium: 480mg
> Magnesium: 49mg Phosphorus: 62mg Iron:
> 1.50mg Copper: 1.49mg Zinc: 0.9mg Selenium:
> 1.8µg Vitamin A: 14µg Beta-carotene: 85µg
> Vitamin B3: 1.15mg Vitamin B6: 0.21mg Vitamin
> B12: 0µg Folic Acid: 56µg Vitamin C: 105mg
> Vitamin E: 1.43mg.

Breakie

The name tells it all. For those of us who cannot face chewing something in the morning this drink is the answer. This rich, creamy drink has plenty of energy-giving B vitamins, which are found in the nuts, and essential carbohydrates from the figs. And ginger is known as a digestive tonic, which helps to prevent nausea.

You can use normal skimmed milk instead of rice milk, if you prefer.

350ml (1¼ cups) of rice milk

2 dried figs

50g (2oz) of almonds and walnuts, ground

4 dried apricots or one fresh one if in season

slice of ginger

sprinkle of nutmeg

Place all the ingredients in the blender and mix until smooth. Makes approximately 400ml (just under 2 cups).

> Energy (kcal): 664 Protein: 12.95g Fat: 36.6g
> Saturated fat: 3.65g Monounsaturated fat: 12.5g
> Polyunsaturated fat: 17.85g Carbohydrates: 76.5g
> Total Sugars: 61.9g Dietary fibre: 18.3g Sodium:
> 203mg Potassium: 1,473mg Calcium: 677mg
> Magnesium: 171mg Phosphorus: 322mg Iron:
> 4.95mg Copper: 0.9mg Zinc: 2.1g Selenium:
> 8.6µg Vitamin A: 795µg Beta-carotene: 288µg
> Vitamin B3: 2.72mg Vitamin B6: 0.38mg Vitamin
> B12: 2.25µg Folic Acid: 38µg Vitamin C: 1mg
> Vitamin E: 6.95mg.

Breakie

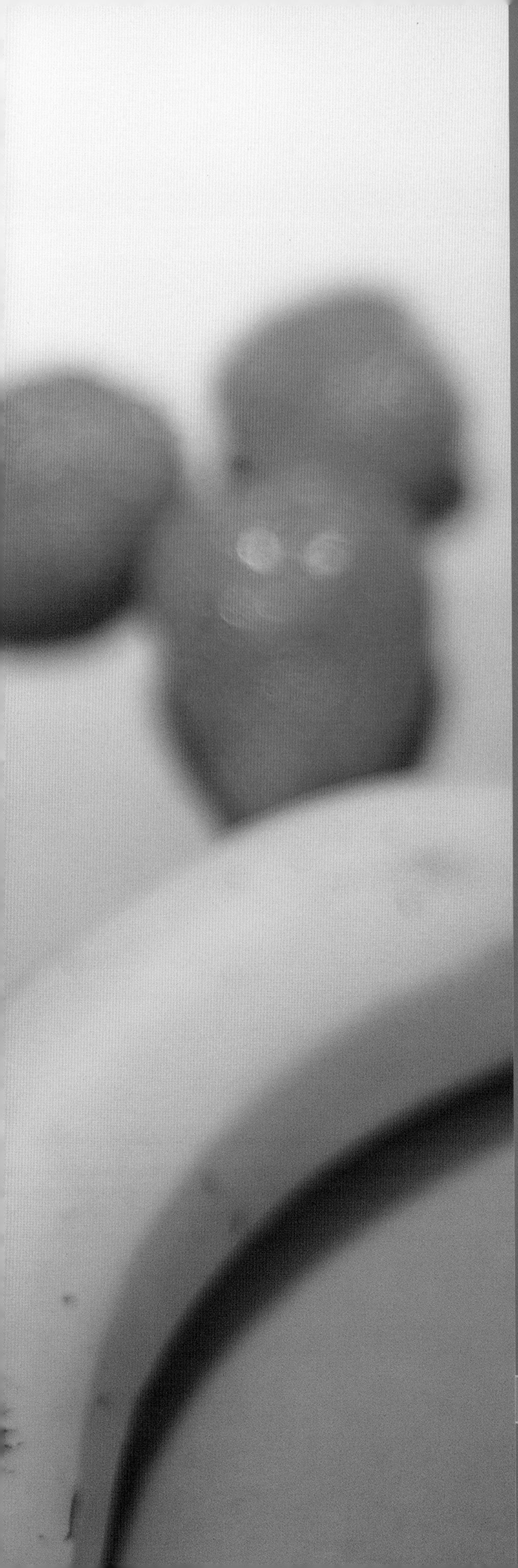

Full Of It

The taste of fresh berries is fantastic, but if they aren't available, you can find a whole selection of frozen ones in your supermarket. This drink is literally full of vital vitamins B, C and E, giving the body a boost of energy, and the minerals potassium, sodium, calcium, magnesium and bioflavonoids. Berries are full of antioxidants, which help to fight off diseases, while the vitamin C content helps to build collagen and so slow down the process of aging.

350g (16oz) berries (I used raspberries, strawberries and blackcurrants)
1 banana, peeled
2 teaspoons of protein powder (you can also enjoy this drink without the protein powder)

Place all the ingredients in a blender and mix until smooth. Drink it slowly and enjoy the rich taste. Makes approximately 350ml (1¼ cups) of juice.

Energy (kcal): 188 Protein: 4.8g Fat: 0.8g Saturated fat: 0.2g Monounsaturated fat: 0.1g Polyunsaturated fat: 0.2g Carbohydrates: 43.2g Total Sugars: 40.9g Dietary fibre: 22.1g Sodium: 15mg Potassium: 1,203mg Calcium: 121mg Magnesium: 88mg Phosphorus: 141mg Iron: 3.05mg Copper: 0.46mg Zinc: 1mg Selenium: 1µg Vitamin A: 25µg Beta-carotene: 148µg Vitamin B3: 2.35mg Vitamin B6: 0.52mg Vitamin B12: 0µg Folic Acid: 78µg Vitamin C: 362mg Vitamin E: 2.19mg.

Full Of It

For Women

Over the past century women's lives have changed to encompass an ever-increasing amount of commitments at work and home every day. So it's no wonder that women need to look after themselves more than ever. Of course, there is an awful lot of reading matter out there about the problems that women face in terms of medical complaints, whether they be large or small.

For instance, you may be one of the many women who suffer from premenstural tension and the usual fluid retention, in which case the vitamin B complex and the minerals calcium, magnesium, iron, potassium and zinc are all helpful. Or you may be experiencing the symptoms of menopause, such as hot flushes, fatigue, chills, or depression and need extra energy, and Breakie (see page 57) is ideal for overcoming any lack of energy you may feel.

Other common problems include cystitis, for which berries, particularly cranberries are recommended – Razzleberry (see page 51) is a good recipe to try for this – and anaemia (a lack of iron in the blood), which you should always consult your doctor about.

Women who are trying for, or expecting, a baby are advised to take folic acid and their diet needs to be rich in nutrients to ensure the optimum health for both mother and baby. If you are pregnant, dilute your power drinks as your digestive system can be more delicate at this time.

Blood Tonic

This sweet, red drink is packed with iron and folic acid. Beetroot juice has been used as a blood-builder and body cleanser in traditional medicine for a long time, while the bean sprouts are also rich in iron and vitamin C, which enables the body to absorb more iron than it would normally if it were not present.

100g (4oz) bean sprouts
2 stalks of celery
½ beetroot
2 medium-sized carrots, topped and tailed
1 teaspoon brahmi powder

Feed all the ingredients, except the brahmi powder, into the juicer. Pour the juice into a glass and stir in the brahmi. Makes approximately 250ml (just over 1¼ cups) of juice.

Energy (kcal): 83 Protein: 4.7g Fat: 1.8g
Saturated fat: 0.4g Monounsaturated fat: 0.1g
Polyunsaturated fat: 1.0g Carbohydrates: 12.6g
Total Sugars: 11.1g Dietary fibre: 7.8g Sodium: 92mg Potassium: 940mg Calcium: 86mg
Magnesium: 17mg Phosphorus: 117mg Iron: 1.48mg Copper: 0.05mg Zinc: 0.7mg Selenium: 3.5µg Vitamin A: 1,126µg Beta-carotene: 6,756µg
Vitamin B3: 0.65mg Vitamin B6: 0.51mg Vitamin B12: 0µg Folic Acid: 185µg Vitamin C: 128mg
Vitamin E: 1.63 mg.

Blood Tonic

Powerful Greens

Another lovely drink which will help fight anaemia, this gorgeous green-coloured, sweet-tasting drink is also packed with iron and folic acid.

Cabbage is part of the cruciferous plant family known for its anti-cancer fighting properties, and cabbage and spinach contain the pigment chlorophyll, which is almost identical to the haemoglobin in our blood so that also helps build up the blood cells. Alfalfa is used for a variety of conditions, due to its high content of vitamins and minerals, so it has lots of benefits.

50g (2oz) alfalfa

3 cabbage leaves

½ beetroot

½ cucumber

150g (6oz) spinach

Feed all the ingredients into a juicer and then pour the juice into a glass. Makes about 350ml (just over 1¼ cups) of juice.

Energy (kcal): 87 Protein: 8.6g Fat: 2.1g
Saturated fat: 0.3g Monounsaturated fat: 0.2g
Polyunsaturated fat: 1.1g Carbohydrates: 8.9g
Total Sugars: 8.5g Dietary fibre: 9.8g Sodium:
231mg Potassium: 1,184mg Calcium: 337mg
Magnesium: 106mg Phosphorus: 162mg Iron:
4.67mg Copper: 0.17mg Zinc: 1.9mg Selenium:
2.7µg Vitamin A: 970µg Beta-carotene: 5,818µg
Vitamin B3: 2.67mg Vitamin B6: 0.48mg Vitamin
B12: 0µg Folic Acid: 360µg Vitamin C: 100mg
Vitamin E: 2.81mg.

Fragile

This great juice is soothing and antispasmodic, ideal for helping the symptoms of premenstrual tension. Many might not like the flavour of fennel but it helps to relax the nerves and contains all the minerals needed during this time of the month. Flaxseed oil provides the body with all the essential fatty acids it needs and is known to be a mood enhancer.

4 medium-sized carrots, topped and tailed

½ bulb of fennel

2 stalks of celery

150g (6oz) spinach

1 teaspoon of flaxseed oil

With the exception of the flaxseed oil, feed all the ingredients into the juicer, pour into a glass and stir in the oil. Makes approximately 350ml (just over 1¼ cups) of juice.

Energy (kcal): 114 Protein: 6.7g Fat: 2.1g
Saturated fat: 0.3g Monounsaturated fat: 0.2g
Polyunsaturated fat: 1.2g Carbohydrates: 18g
Total Sugars: 16.9g Dietary fibre: 11.4g Sodium:
317mg Potassium: 1,838mg Calcium: 361mg
Magnesium: 100mg Phosphorus: 142mg Iron:
4.35mg Copper: 0.12mg Zinc: 1.9mg Selenium:
5.8µg Vitamin A: 3,083µg Beta-carotene:
18,500µg Vitamin B3: 3.11mg Vitamin B6: 0.58mg
Vitamin B12: 0µg Folic Acid: 309µg Vitamin C:
62mg Vitamin E: 3.64mg.

Peachy

Wonderfully sweet with a sharp aftertaste of ginger Peachy is another great treat for those of you who feel under the weather when pregnant.

3 peaches (use tinned peaches if not in
      season)
slice of peeled ginger

Place all the ingredients in a blender and mix until smooth. Makes approximately 200ml (just under a cup).

> **Energy (kcal): 96 Protein: 1.5g Fat: 0g Saturated fat: 0.0g Monounsaturated fat: 0.0g Polyunsaturated fat: 0.0g Carbohydrates: 23.7g Total Sugars: 23.3g Dietary fibre: 2.2g Sodium: 29mg Potassium: 423mg Calcium: 11mg Magnesium: 17mg Phosphorus: 46mg Iron: 1.02mg Copper: 0.10mg Zinc: 0.2mg Selenium: 0µg Vitamin A: 27µg Beta-carotene:163µg Vitamin B3: 1.52mg Vitamin B6: 0.05mg Vitamin B12: 0µg Folic Acid: 5µg Vitamin C: 15mg Vitamin E: 0mg.**

Groovy Chick

One of my favourite drinks, as it is so refreshing and the ginger gives it a great extra flavour, Groovy Chick is brilliant for anyone who is pregnant. The ginger is known to prevent morning sickness and so the perfect ingredient in this drink.

You could also try Caramba (see page 55) and Replenish (see page 57). The pears in that are a great source of folic acid and essential vitamins and minerals

5 medium-sized carrots, topped and tailed
2 apples, quartered
slice of peeled ginger (size according to your
      taste).

Feed all the ingredients into a juicer.and then pour the juice into a glass. Makes approximately 300ml (1¼ cups) of juice.

> **Energy (kcal): 298 Protein: 13.9g Fat: 4.8g Saturated fat: 2.5g Monounsaturated fat: 0.0g Polyunsaturated fat: 0.5g Carbohydrates: 53g Total Sugars: 35.4g Dietary fibre: 8.2g Sodium: 246mg Potassium: 543mg Calcium: 465mg Magnesium: 55mg Phosphorus: 372mg Iron: 1.01mg Copper: 0.07mg Zinc: 2.4mg Selenium: 1.6µg Vitamin A: 2,207µg Beta-carotene: 13,025µg Vitamin B3: 0.69mg Vitamin B6: 0.34mg Vitamin B12: 0µg Folic Acid: 46µg Vitamin C: 24mg Vitamin E: 2.08mg.**

Femme Fatale

Another great refreshing drink that is particularly good for anyone suffering from premenstrual tension, the flaxseed oil in Femme Fatale provides essential fatty acids while the ginger give this drink its kick.

slice of peeled ginger

½ bulb of fennel

3 medium-sized carrots, topped and tailed

½ cucumber

1 apple, quartered

Beginning with the ginger, feed all the ingredients into the juicer and then pour the juice into a glass. Makes approximately 400ml (just less than 2 cups) of juice.

Energy (kcal): 108 Protein: 2.4g Fat: 0.7g
Saturated fat: 0.1g Monounsaturated fat: 0.0g
Polyunsaturated fat: 0.3g Carbohydrates: 24.2g
Total Sugars: 23.1g Dietary fibre: 5.8g Sodium:
43mg Potassium: 743mg Calcium: 67mg
Magnesium: 21mg Phosphorus: 94mg Iron:
1.0mg Copper: 0.07mg Zinc: 0.6mg Selenium:
1.2µg Vitamin A: 1,650µg Beta-carotene: 9,903µg
Vitamin B3: 0.98mg Vitamin B6: 0.30mg Vitamin
B12: 0µg Folic Acid: 50µg Vitamin C: 18mg
Vitamin E: 1.33mg.

Tropicana

A delightful fruity drink full of bone-building minerals and vitamin C and beta-carotene with strong antioxidant properties, Tropicana is excellent for anyone who is pregnant.

½ papaya, peeled and diced

1 banana, peeled and diced

1 orange, peeled and diced, pips removed

Place all the ingredients in a blender and mix until smooth. To dilute this drink just add some still or sparkling water. Makes approximately 250ml (just under a cup).

Energy (kcal): 187 Protein: 4g Fat: 0.6g
Saturated fat: 0.6g Monounsaturated fat: 0.1g
Polyunsaturated fat: 0.0g Carbohydrates: 43.4g
Total Sugars: 34.5g Dietary fibre: 7.8g Sodium:
27mg Potassium: 892mg Calcium: 121mg
Magnesium: 117mg Phosphorus: 98mg Iron:
1.18mg Copper: 0.30mg Zinc: 0.6mg Selenium:
2.6µg Vitamin A: 12µg Beta-carotene: 74µg
Vitamin B3: 1.58mg Vitamin B6: 0.45mg Vitamin
B12: 0µg Folic Acid: 64µg Vitamin C: 104mg
Vitamin E: 0.65mg.

Femme Fatale

Potassium Loader

Great for relieving fluid retention, the high content of potassium and sodium in Potassium loader helps to regulate the amount of water in the body. Celery and spinach also contain the bone-building minerals calcium and magnesium.

4 medium-sized carrots, topped and tailed
2 stalks of celery
100g (4oz) of spinach
some parsley

Feed all the ingredients into the juicer and then pour into a glass. Makes approximately 300ml (1¼ cups) of juice.

> Energy (kcal): 89 Protein: 4.3g Fat: 1.5g
> Saturated fat: 0.3g Monounsaturated fat: 0.1g
> Polyunsaturated fat: 0.9g Carbohydrates: 15.2g
> Total Sugars: 14.2g Dietary fibre: 9.8g Sodium: 235mg Potassium: 1,089mg Calcium: 254mg
> Magnesium: 64mg Phosphorus: 90mg Iron: 3.23mg Copper: 0.08mg Zinc: 1.0mg Selenium: 5.3µg Vitamin A: 2,786µg Beta-carotene: 16,717µg Vitamin B3: 1.83mg Vitamin B6: 0.42mg Vitamin B12: 0µg Folic Acid: 190µg Vitamin C: 50mg Vitamin E: 2.85mg.

Cool Mint

The watermelon in this drink is an excellent source of potassium with its diuretic properties, which makes it very helpful in combating fluid retention, and it is also really refreshing and tasty. Together with the cucumber, watermelon provides our bodies with vitamins A and C giving skin a healthy glow at the same time.

1 slice of watermelon, peeled and diced
½ cucumber, peeled and diced
some fresh mint (according to preference)

Place all the ingredients in a blender and mix until smooth. Makes approximately 350ml (just over 1¼ cups) of juice.

> Energy (kcal): 64 Protein: 1.2g Fat: 0.6g
> Saturated fat: 0.2g Monounsaturated fat: 0.2g
> Polyunsaturated fat: 0.2g Carbohydrates: 14.4g
> Total Sugars: 14.2g Dietary fibre: 0.6g Sodium: 5mg Potassium: 214mg Calcium: 22mg
> Magnesium: 16mg Phosphorus: 22mg Iron: 0.97mg Copper: 0.06mg Zinc: 0.4mg Selenium: 0µg Vitamin A: 82µg Beta-carotene: 480µg Vitamin B3: 0.25mg Vitamin B6: 0.28mg Vitamin B12: 0µg Folic Acid: 8µg Vitamin C: 17mg Vitamin E: 0.39mg.

Cool Mint

For Men

Men are just as much in need of a boost sometimes as women. So, these drinks are aimed at alleviating some of the more common ailments that men suffer.

Ready Steady

The ingredients in this drink really help to cleanse the prostate and sex glands.

5 medium-sized carrots, topped and tailed
½ beetroot
½ cucumber

Feed all the ingredients into the juicer and pour the juice in to a glass. Makes approximately 250ml (just under a cup).

Energy (kcal): 77 Protein: 1.5g Fat: 0.6g
Saturated fat: 0.2g Monounsaturated fat: 0.0g
Polyunsaturated fat: 0.4g Carbohydrates: 17.2g
Total Sugars: 16.1g Dietary fibre: 5.7g Sodium:
62mg Potassium: 411mg Calcium: 54mg
Magnesium: 8mg Phosphorus: 40mg Iron:
0.78mg Copper: 0.04mg Zinc: 0.3mg Selenium:
2.0µg Vitamin A: 2,706µg Beta-carotene:
16,235µg Vitamin B3: 0.42mg Vitamin B6:
0.29mg Vitamin B12: 0µg Folic Acid: 51µg
Vitamin C: 13mg Vitamin E: 1.12mg.

Iron Man

Iron Man

You won't quite be bending bars with this, but it is a great source of iron, keeping blood cells supplied with oxygen and the bone-building minerals calcium and magnesium. Iron Man is also a very good source of the vitamins A, B complex, C and full of beta-carotene to boost the immune system.

6 florets of broccoli
150g (6oz) spinach, thoroughly washed
1 red pepper, stalk removed and deseeded
½ apple for sweetness (use 1
      apple if it is not sweet enough),
      peeled, cored and diced
1 teaspoon bee pollen

Feed the spinach, pepper and apple into the juicer leaving the apple until last, as it is a harder fruit, which will help to extract any juices left over in the juicer. Pour the juice into a glass and stir in the bee pollen. Makes approximately 400ml (just under 2 cups) of juice.

Energy (kcal): 222 Protein: 18.3g Fat: 4.5g
Saturated fat: 0.9g Monounsaturated fat: 0.4g
Polyunsaturated fat: 2.6g Carbohydrates: 28g
Total Sugars: 26.4g Dietary fibre: 7.0g Sodium:
242mg Potassium: 2,149mg Calcium: 425mg
Magnesium: 172mg Phosphorus: 354mg Iron:
8.41mg Copper: 0.15mg Zinc: 2.9mg Selenium:
1.5µg Vitamin A: 2,425µg Beta-carotene:
14,547µg Vitamin B3: 6.90mg Vitamin B6: 1.39mg
Vitamin B12: 0µg Folic Acid: 511µg Vitamin C:
558mg Vitamin E: 8.07mg.

Berry Mania

Packed with protein, Berry Mania will really help build up muscles and the vitamin C is good for the immune system and is also an antioxidant.

250g (10oz) strawberries and raspberries

1 banana, peeled and diced

2 tablespoons whey powder

Place all the ingredients in a blender and mix until smooth. Makes approximately 300ml (1¼ cups).

Energy (kcal): 160 Protein: 4g Fat: 0.8g
Saturated fat: 0.2g Monounsaturated fat: 0.1g
Polyunsaturated fat: 0.2g Carbohydrates: 36.5g
Total Sugars: 34.1g Dietary fibre: 14.0g Sodium:
12mg Potassium: 812mg Calcium: 57mg
Magnesium: 70mg Phosphorus: 97mg Iron:
1.67mg Copper: 0.31mg Zinc: 0.7mg Selenium:
1.0µg Vitamin A: 6µg Beta-carotene: 38µg
Vitamin B3: 2.08mg Vitamin B6: 0.44mg Vitamin
B12: 0µg Folic Acid: 80µg Vitamin C: 147mg
Vitamin E: 1.12mg.

Tropical Beach

OK, so who hasn't suffered from a hangover at some point? Well, this drink will certainly help put back the vitamin C that has been lost and it is also essential to protect your immune system. The potassium will restore your fluid balance and the vitamin B1 found in the oranges helps to process alcohol through your system.

2 oranges, peeled if desired (see below)

1 banana, peeled and diced

100ml (half a cup) coconut milk

½ lime, peeled and pips removed

You can either peel the orange and place it in the blender or use a citrus press to extract the juice and then mix it with the other ingredients in the blender. Makes approximately 600ml (2½ cups).

Energy (kcal): 490 Protein: 8.4g Fat: 25.9g
Saturated fat: 22.3g Monounsaturated fat: 2g
Polyunsaturated fat: 0.0g Carbohydrates: 60.7g
Total Sugars: 53.2g Dietary fibre: 8.9g Sodium:
128mg Potassium: 1,195mg Calcium: 208mg
Magnesium: 99mg Phosphorus: 230mg Iron:
2.43mg Copper: 0.31mg Zinc: 0.6mg Selenium:
4.2µg Vitamin A: 19µg Beta-carotene: 114µg
Vitamin B3: 2.93mg Vitamin B6: 0.66mg Vitamin
B12: 0µg Folic Acid: 115µg Vitamin C: 200mg
Vitamin E: 1.04mg.

Diamond White

Overeating, eating too fast or eating a lot of rich food can all lead to indigestion. This zesty drink will help as the pineapple contains an enzyme called bromelin, which helps with digestive problems, while the banana contains potassium, which helps to regulate the body's fluid balance.

1 pineapple, peeled and diced
1 banana, peeled and diced
1 orange, peeled and diced, pips removed
150g (6oz) white seedless grapes

Put all the ingredients in the blender and mix until smooth. If you find the consistency is too thick, add some still or sparkling water during blending. Makes approximately 400ml (just under 2 cups) of juice.

> **Energy (kcal): 292 Protein: 4.1g Fat: 0.9g**
> **Saturated fat: 0.1g Polyunsaturated fat: 0.2g**
> **Monounsaturated fat: 0.3g Carbohydrates: 71.4g**
> **Total Sugars: 69.1g Dietary fibre: 9.0g Sodium:**
> **15mg Potassium: 1,148mg Calcium: 126mg**
> **Magnesium: 84mg Phosphorus: 99mg Iron:**
> **1.14mg Copper: 0.50mg Zinc: 0.6mg Selenium:**
> **3.8μg Vitamin A: 19μg Beta-carotene: 115μg**
> **Vitamin B3: 2.06mg Vitamin B6: 0.71mg Vitamin**
> **B12: 0μg Folic Acid: 74μg Vitamin C: 120mg**
> **Vitamin E: 0.81mg.**

Delightful

It may seem an odd combination, but the taste of this drink really does live up to its name. Cabbage has been attributed with healing properties and helps to neutralise stomach acids, while apples contain many essential minerals and are a good source of dietary fibre and have been found to help reduce cholesterol levels.

200g (8oz) white cabbage
2 apples, quartered

Feed the ingredients into the juicer and pour the juice into a glass. Makes approximately 250ml (1 cup) of juice.

> **Energy (kcal): 146 Protein: 4.2g Fat: 1.0g**
> **Saturated fat: 0.2g Monounsaturated fat: 0.0g**
> **Polyunsaturated fat: 0.8g Carbohydrates: 31.8g**
> **Total Sugars: 31.6g Dietary fibre: 9.8g Sodium:**
> **16mg Potassium: 780mg Calcium: 112mg**
> **Magnesium: 26mg Phosphorus: 104mg Iron:**
> **1.60mg Copper: 0.08mg Zinc: 0.8mg Selenium:**
> **2.0μg Vitamin A: 134μg Beta-carotene: 806μg**
> **Vitamin B3: 1.20mg Vitamin B6: 0.46mg Vitamin**
> **B12: 0μg Folic Acid: 152μg Vitamin C: 110mg**
> **Vitamin E: 1.58mg.**

For Children and Young Adults

Children can be fussy eaters and juices offer a great way to give them the essential vitamins and minerals they need. However, their digestive systems are more delicate, so dilute the juices with water and give them smaller quantities and build up their consumption slowly. The following recipes are especially devised for small tummies!

Avocado Cream

A yummy creamy drink, full of essential B vitamins, Avocado Cream will really help boost energy and aid normal growth and development.

½ ripe avocado, peeled, stoned and diced
1 banana, peeled and diced
150ml (⅔ cup) soya milk

Place all the ingredients in the blender and mix until smooth. Makes approximately 200ml (just under cup).

> **Energy (kcal): 413 Protein: 7.6g Fat: 13.2g**
> **Saturated fat: 0.6g Monounsaturated fat: 7.35g**
> **Polyunsaturated fat: 4.4g Carbohydrates: 25.1g**
> **Total Sugars: 21.45g Dietary fibre: 5.2g Sodium: 25mg Potassium: 856mg Calcium: 132mg**
> **Magnesium: 88mg Phosphorus: 128mg Iron: 1.45mg Copper: 0.39mg Zinc: 0.77mg Selenium: 3.12μg Vitamin A: 9μg Beta-carotene: 81μg**
> **Vitamin B3: 1.49mg Vitamin B6: 0.53mg Vitamin B12: 0.75μg Folic Acid: 21μg Vitamin C: 14mg Vitamin E: 7.50mg.**

Scrumptious

Pears are a good source of dietary fibre and contain folic acid, which is essential for a baby's normal development. The avocado is rich in B vitamins and so a very good source of nutrition too.

½ ripe avocado, stoned and peeled
1 pear, cored and diced
150ml (⅔ cup) soya milk

Place all the ingredients in the blender and mix until smooth. Makes approximately 200ml (just under a cup).

> **Energy (kcal): 402 Protein: 7g Fat: 13.1g**
> **Saturated fat: 2.7g Monounsaturated fat: 7.35g**
> **Polyunsaturated fat: 4.3g Carbohydrates: 22.9g**
> **Total Sugars: 21.5g Dietary fibre: 0g Sodium: 30mg Potassium: 771mg Calcium: 149mg**
> **Magnesium: 58mg Phosphorus: 127mg Iron: 1.56mg Copper: 0.41mg Zinc: 0.77mg Selenium: 2.12μg Vitamin A: 12μg Beta-carotene: 98μg**
> **Vitamin B3: 1.22mg Vitamin B6: 0.28mg Vitamin B12: 0.75μg Folic Acid: 12μg Vitamin C: 16mg Vitamin E: 8.28mg.**

Scrumptious

Power Juice

Good for children of school age as it replenishes the energy they use, this drink is a case of power by name and by nature. It contains all the vital minerals – potassium, calcium and iron – as well as vitamin C and beta-carotene.

Another good energy booster is The Kid (see page 41)

1 medium-sized carrot topped and tailed
½ orange, peeled, diced and pips removed
½ banana, peeled and diced
1 dried apricot
100ml (½ cup) semi-skimmed milk

Feed the carrot through the juicer and then add the juice to the blender with the remaining ingredients and mix until smooth. Makes approximately 200ml (just under a cup).

> **Energy (kcal): 202 Protein: 6.6g Fat: 2.3g**
> **Saturated fat: 1.2g Monounsaturated fat: 0.5g**
> **Polyunsaturated fat: 0.1g Carbohydrates: 41.4g**
> **Total Sugars: 39.7g Dietary fibre: 8.2g Sodium:**
> **74mg Potassium: 914mg Calcium: 208mg**
> **Magnesium: 57mg Phosphorus: 160mg Iron:**
> **1.06mg Copper: 0.20mg Zinc: 0.8g Selenium:**
> **4.4µg Vitamin A: 603µg Beta-carotene: 3,380µg**
> **Vitamin B3: 1.59mg Vitamin B6: 0.48mg Vitamin**
> **B12: 0.2µg Folic Acid: 67µg Vitamin C: 96mg**
> **Vitamin E: 0.82mg.**

Playful

Even children can occasionally suffer from constipation, so apples provide a good source of dietary fibre and prunes have laxative properties.

1 apple, peeled, cored and diced
100g (4oz) blackcurrants
3 prunes
a little water

Place all the ingredients in the blender, including the water, which is better added a little at a time so that you can check the consistency, and mix until smooth. Makes approximately 175ml (about ½ a cup).

> **Energy (kcal): 126 Protein: 2g Fat: 0.2g**
> **Saturated fat: 0.0g Monounsaturated fat: 0.0g**
> **Polyunsaturated fat: 0.1g Carbohydrates: 30.9g**
> **Total Sugars: 30.9g Dietary fibre: 10.6g Sodium:**
> **7mg Potassium: 568mg Calcium: 41mg**
> **Magnesium: 26mg Phosphorus: 65mg Iron:**
> **6.17mg Copper: 0.11mg Zinc: 0.3mg Selenium:**
> **0.9µg Vitamin A: 16µg Beta-carotene: 94µg**
> **Vitamin B3: 0.75mg Vitamin B6: 0.24mg Vitamin**
> **B12: 0µg Folic Acid: 6µg Vitamin C: 43mg**
> **Vitamin E: 1.13mg.**

Playful

Bright Eyes

A delicious drink full of beta-carotene and vitamin A, which is essential for eyes to develop properly and keep their sparkle.

2 medium-sized carrots, topped and tailed
1 apple, peeled, cored and diced
125g (5oz) plain yoghurt with live cultures

Feed the ingredients into the juicer and then mix the juice with the yoghurt until it the texture is smooth and creamy. Makes approximately 300ml (1¼ cups).

**Energy (kcal): 145 Protein: 7.3g Fat: 1.3g
Saturated fat: 0.7g Monounsaturated fat: 0.2g
Polyunsaturated fat: 0.3g Carbohydrates: 27.5g
Total Sugars: 27.1g Dietary fibre: 4.1g Sodium:
127mg Potassium: 568mg Calcium: 262mg
Magnesium: 31mg Phosphorus: 223mg Iron:
0.47mg Copper: 0.04mg Zinc: 0.9mg Selenium:
2.0µg Vitamin A: 2,106µg Beta-carotene: 6,516µg
Vitamin B3: 0.39mg Vitamin B6: 0.28mg Vitamin
B12: 0.2µg Folic Acid: 32µg Vitamin C: 12mg
Vitamin E: 1.05mg.**

Chocolate

Who could resist this delicious rich drink? High in potassium and essential B vitamins, no one would suspect the goodness it contains.

50g (2oz) sesame seeds
1 banana, peeled
200ml (just under a cup) water
2 tablespoons of carob
few drops of almond extract

Grind the sesame seeds and place them together with the other ingredients in a blender. Mix until smooth. Makes approximately 300ml (1¼ cups).

**Energy (kcal): 465 Protein: 11g Fat: 33.2g
Saturated fat: 6.6g Monounsaturated fat: 12.1g
Polyunsaturated fat: 13g Carbohydrates: 32.5g
Total Sugars: 29.9g Dietary fibre: 3.1g Sodium:
12mg Potassium: 727mg Calcium: 346mg
Magnesium: 231mg Phosphorus: 408mg Iron:
5.82mg Copper: 0.93mg Zinc: 3.0mg Selenium:
1.6µg Vitamin A: 8µg Beta-carotene: 26µg
Vitamin B3: 3.26mg Vitamin B6: 0.67mg Vitamin
B12: 0µg Folic Acid: 64µg Vitamin C: 11mg
Vitamin E: 1.74mg.**

Chocolate

Under the Weather

There are always times when you just do not feel yourself. Maybe you feel run down and need a boost, or perhaps you are simply overworked, tired or have overdone it a bit. Perhaps you are feeling some of the more common problems associated with aging, such as arthritis or rheumatism. Whatever it is, your body will usually need help in balancing out its vitamins and mineral levels and the recipes here always take account of the restorative properties of their ingredients. So, for example, lettuce will be used to help induce sleep, while pineapple will be used to help with poor digestion.

In this section, you will find drinks to combat stress and anxiety, or cope with insomnia and fatigue, or alleviate varicose veins, as well as help bruises to heal. And there are drinks to relieve sore throats, coughs and bronchitis and ideas for pick-me-ups to give a little zest to a flagging sex drive, even recipes to help bruises to heal more quickly.

Whether you suffer from the embarrassment of wind or need something light to counteract the symptoms of depression, Under the Weather will have a recipe or two which will put you back on the road to recovery and give you a great tasting drink along the way.

Free Falling

Free Falling

Do you have a temperature, do you ache all over? Try this delicious sweet drink: it's sure to get you back up and fighting fit. Full of anti-inflammatory enzymes plus lots of vitamin C to boost your immune system, the grapes in this drink are an excellent source of B vitamins, which will give essential energy to fight a fever, and the potassium also found in the grapes and the melon will restore your water balance and help your body to flush out toxins.

125g (5oz) white seedless grapes

1 pear, cored and diced

½ cantaloupe melon, peeled, diced and
    deseeded

2 teaspoons guarana powder

Place all the ingredients in the blender and mix until smooth. Makes approximately 400ml (just less than 2 cups) of juice. Drink slowly and enjoy.

> Energy (kcal): 190 Protein: 2g Fat: 0.5g
> Saturated fat: 0.0g Monounsaturated fat: 0.0g
> Polyunsaturated fat: 0.0g Carbohydrates: 47.3g
> Total Sugars: 47.3g Dietary fibre: 2.4g Sodium:
> 21mg Potassium: 903mg Calcium: 70mg
> Magnesium: 40mg Phosphorus: 70mg Iron:
> 1.26mg Copper: 0.28mg Zinc: 0.3mg Selenium:
> 1.3µg Vitamin A: 260µg Beta-carotene: 1,560µg
> Vitamin B3: 1.58mg Vitamin B6: 0.34mg Vitamin
> B12: 0µg Folic Acid: 14µg Vitamin C: 56mg
> Vitamin E: 1.20mg.

Delirious

Here's another great drink packed with anti-inflammatory enzymes and vitamin C to get you out of bed. Strawberries contain a natural painkiller, an aspirin-like substance, and are used to treat fevers and pomegranates are teeming with immune-boosting vitamin C.

1 pomegranate, peeled
1 orange, peeled, diced, pips removed
150g (6oz) strawberries
150g (6oz) red grapes

Place all the ingredients in the blender and mix until smooth. Add some water if the consistency is too thick for your liking. Makes approximately 500ml (2¼ cups).

Energy (kcal): 200 Protein: 3.8g Fat: 0.5g Saturated fat: 0.6g Monounsaturated fat: 0.0g Polyunsaturated fat: 0.0g Carbohydrates: 48.1g Total Sugars: 48.1g Dietary fibre: 7.1g Sodium: 20mg Potassium: 843mg Calcium: 121mg Magnesium: 44mg Phosphorus: 102mg Iron: 1.35mg Copper: 0.40mg Zinc: 0.5mg Selenium: 3.1µg Vitamin A: 15µg Beta-carotene: 89µg Vitamin B3: 1.90mg Vitamin B6: 0.46mg Vitamin B12: 0µg Folic Acid: 83µg Vitamin C: 209mg Vitamin E: 0.68mg.

Immune Booster

A refreshing juice containing echinacea, a herb that is known for its immune strengthening properties, the carrots and orange in Immune Booster are full of vitamin C and beta-carotene which will help the body fight infections, while the ginger is useful in combating colds.

slice of peeled ginger
3 medium-sized carrots, topped and tailed
1 apple, quartered
1 orange, quartered
20 drops of echinacea

Feed the ginger first into the juicer and then the carrots, apple and orange. Pour the juice into a glass and stir in the echinacea. Makes approximately 370ml (just under 1½ cups).

Energy (kcal): 150 Protein: 3g Fat: 0.7g Saturated fat: 0.1g Monounsaturated fat: 0.0g Polyunsaturated fat: 0.3g Carbohydrates: 35.3g Total Sugars: 34.3g Dietary fibre: 8.0g Sodium: 41mg Potassium: 579mg Calcium: 110mg Magnesium: 25mg Phosphorus: 63mg Iron: 0.68mg Copper: 0.12mg Zinc: 0.4mg Selenium: 2.8µg Vitamin A: 1,634µg Beta-carotene: 9,803µg Vitamin B3: 1.06mg Vitamin B6: 0.39mg Vitamin B12: 0µg Folic Acid: 65µg Vitamin C: 100mg Vitamin E: 1.65mg.

Delirious

Respirator

A great drink to relieve coughs and bronchitis, the cool mango in Respirator is full of immune-boosting vitamin C and beta-carotene. In addition, the mint has antispasmodic and anti-inflammatory properties, which should also help settle chests.

1 mango, peeled, stoned and diced
250ml (about a cup) rice milk
some mint leaves

Put all the ingredients together in the blender and mix until smooth. Makes approximately 350ml (just over 1¼ cups) of juice.

> **Energy (kcal): 260 Protein: 2.05g Fat: 3g
> Saturated fat: 0.45g Monounsaturated fat: 0.5g
> Polyunsaturated fat: 1.75g Carbohydrates: 59g
> Total Sugars: 48.5g Dietary fibre: 7.0g Sodium:
> 5mg Potassium: 442mg Calcium: 337mg
> Magnesium: 31mg Phosphorus: 41mg Iron:
> 2.04mg Copper: 0.29mg Zinc: 0.2mg Selenium:
> 0µg Vitamin A: 1,225µg Beta-carotene: 4,348µg
> Vitamin B3: 1.24mg Vitamin B6: 0.31mg Vitamin
> B12: 1.5µg Folic Acid: 4µg Vitamin C: 90mg
> Vitamin E: 2.71mg.**

Rocky

This drinking is rocking with vitamin C to boost your immune system as the raspberries, orange and kiwi all are high in vitamin C and potassium. Oranges and kiwi are good sources of dietary fibre and so help reduce cholesterol levels, while yoghurt is soothing to the digestive system.

150g (6oz) raspberries
1 orange, peeled, diced, pips removed
½ teaspoon of vitamin C powder (provides you with a 1000mg dose, the body cannot absorb more than this at a time.)
1 kiwi, peeled and diced
125g (5oz) plain yoghurt with live culture

You can use a citrus press to extract the juice of the orange, if you prefer a smoother drink. Otherwise, place all the ingredients in the blender and mix until smooth. Makes approximately 350ml (just over 1¼ cups).

> **Energy (kcal): 196 Protein: 10.9g Fat: 1.9g
> Saturated fat: 0.8g Monounsaturated fat: 0.4g
> Polyunsaturated fat: 0.2g Carbohydrates: 36.2g
> Total Sugars: 36.1g Dietary fibre: 12.9g Sodium:
> 119mg Potassium: 982mg Calcium: 365mg
> Magnesium: 77mg Phosphorus: 299mg Iron:
> 1.58mg Copper: 0.31mg Zinc: 1.4mg Selenium:
> 2.8µg Vitamin A: 34µg Beta-carotene: 82µg
> Vitamin B3: 1.70mg Vitamin B6: 0.45mg Vitamin
> B12: 0.2µg Folic Acid: 120µg Vitamin C: 1,171mg
> Vitamin E: 1.12mg.**

Rocky

Mint Apple

Also good for coughs, this refreshing drink is full of vitamin C to boost the immune system and beta-carotene with its antioxidant properties. Pineapples are known to be used for treating bronchitis amongst other conditions and mint has anti-inflammatory and anti-bacterial properties.

1 pineapple, peeled and diced
½ mango, peeled, stoned and diced
some fresh mint
100ml (1/2 cup) water

Place all the ingredients in the blender and mix until smooth. If you it is still too thick for your liking, add some extra still or sparkling water. Makes approximately 400ml (just under 2 cups).

Energy (kcal): 266 Protein: 2.8g Fat: 1.2g
Saturated fat: 0.1g Monounsaturated fat: 0.5g
Polyunsaturated fat: 0.5g Carbohydrates: 65.5g
Total Sugars: 65g Dietary fibre: 9.7g Sodium:
12mg Potassium: 989mg Calcium: 105mg
Magnesium: 92mg Phosphorus: 69mg Iron:
1.98mg Copper: 0.67mg Zinc: 0.6mg Selenium:
0µg Vitamin A: 377µg Beta-carotene: 2,260µg
Vitamin B3: 2.06mg Vitamin B6: 0.59mg Vitamin
B12: 0µg Folic Acid: 26µg Vitamin C: 103mg
Vitamin E: 1.83mg.

Red Devil

This delicious red drink has great decongestant properties. The beetroot and radish will help to protect the mucous membrane and there is also lots of vitamin C to boost the immune system.

½ cucumber, peeled and diced
100g (4oz) radish
½ beetroot
½ red pepper, stalk removed and
        deseeded

Feed all the ingredients into the juicer and then pour the juice into a glass. Makes approximately 400ml (just under 2 cups) of juice.

Energy (kcal): 51 Protein: 2g Fat: 0.6g Saturated
fat: 0.6g Monounsaturated fat: 0.0g
Polyunsaturated fat: 0.3g Carbohydrates: 9.7g
Total Sugars: 9.3g Dietary fibre: 3.3g Sodium:
27mg Potassium: 471mg Calcium: 31mg
Magnesium: 21mg Phosphorus: 52mg Iron:
1.08mg Copper: 0.02mg Zinc: 0.4mg Selenium:
2µg Vitamin A: 641µg Beta-carotene: 3,845µg
Vitamin B3: 1.72mg Vitamin B6: 0.44mg Vitamin
B12: 0µg Folic Acid: 86µg Vitamin C: 158mg
Vitamin E: 0.80mg.

Mint Apple

Hot Stuff

Feel the soothing and anti-bacterial action in this sharp fresh tasting juice which is full of vitamin C to boost your immune system. Radishes and garlic are very beneficial to the lungs, and will sooth and cleanse the whole body.

You could also try Grease Lightning (see page 49) which will have the same effect.

2 tomatoes, quartered

2 stalks of celery

100g (4oz) radishes

2 medium-sized carrots, topped and tailed

slice of peeled ginger

½ clove of garlic, peeled

some black pepper

Feed all the ingredients, except the pepper, into the juicer, starting with the garlic and ginger. Add pepper to taste. Makes approximately 300ml (1¼ cups) of juice.

> Energy (kcal): 75 Protein: 3.3g Fat: 1.2g
> Saturated fat: 0.3g Monounsaturated fat: 0.1g
> Polyunsaturated fat: 0.6g Carbohydrates: 14.2g
> Total Sugars: 12.7g Dietary fibre: 6.1g Sodium:
> 98mg Potassium: 1,069mg Calcium: 98mg
> Magnesium: 27mg Phosphorus: 95mg Iron:
> 2.31mg Copper: 0.08mg Zinc: 0.6mg Selenium:
> 5.7µg Vitamin A: 1,229µg Beta-carotene: 7,375µg
> Vitamin B3: 2.26mg Vitamin B6: 0.41mg Vitamin
> B12: 0µg Folic Acid: 84µg Vitamin C: 52mg
> Vitamin E: 2.21mg.

Ginger Rogers

Ginger has many medicinal actions, and it is frequently used as an important ingredient in Chinese medicine because it really helps to stimulate all the body's functions. Full of vital vitamins A and C, Ginger Rogers should really put a bit of spice in your sex life!

4 medium-sized carrots, topped and tailed

2 apples, quartered

1 small fresh root of ginger

Feed all the ingredients into a juicer, then pour the juice into a glass. Makes approximately 350ml (just over 1¼ cups) of juice.

> Energy (kcal): 154 Protein: 1.9g Fat: 0.8g
> Saturated fat: 0.2g Monounsaturated fat: 0.0g
> Polyunsaturated fat: 0.5g Carbohydrates: 37g
> Total Sugars: 35.4g Dietary fibre: 8.2g Sodium:
> 47mg Potassium: 543mg Calcium: 50mg
> Magnesium: 15mg Phosphorus: 46mg Iron:
> 0.81mg Copper: 0.07mg Zinc: 0.4mg Selenium:
> 1.6µg Vitamin A: 2,171µg Beta-carotene:
> 13,025µg Vitamin B3: 0.69mg Vitamin B6:
> 0.34mg Vitamin B12: 0µg Folic Acid: 21µg
> Vitamin C: 22mg Vitamin E: 2.08mg.

Hot Stuff

Green Living

With the soothing and sedative properties of the lettuce and the cooling effect of the cucumber this is a delicious combination for a sore throat.

6 lettuce leaves, thoroughly washed

1 stalk celery

½ cucumber

2 apples, quartered

½ lime

6 cabbage leaves, thoroughly washed

Feed all the ingredients into the juicer. Makes approximately 450ml (2 cups) of juice.

Energy (kcal): 175 Protein: 6.1g Fat: 1.8g Saturated fat: 0.6g Monounsaturated fat: 0.0g Polyunsaturated fat: 1.3g Carbohydrates: 35.4g Total Sugars: 35.2g Dietary fibre: 12.7g Sodium: 46mg Potassium: 1,243mg Calcium: 174mg Magnesium: 39mg Phosphorus: 159mg Iron: 2.64mg Copper: 0.11mg Zinc: 1.2mg Selenium: 4.5µg Vitamin A: 202µg Beta-carotene: 1,214µg Vitamin B3: 2.06mg Vitamin B6: 0.59mg Vitamin B12: 0µg Folic Acid: 235µg Vitamin C: 149mg Vitamin E: 2.20mg.

Green Living

Ruby Red

A drink that is sure to get you looking on the bright side of life no matter what's been getting you down, Ruby Red is great for raising the spirits. A deep red colour, it is full of essential fatty acids which are contained in the sunflower and pumpkin seeds. You can add a teaspoon of flaxseed oil, if you like as it also contains these fatty acids and has little taste. Ruby Red is also packed with B vitamins, which help the nervous system and provide energy.

3 tomatoes, quartered

100g (4oz) radishes

½ clove of garlic

25g (1oz) parsley

50g (2oz) of ground sunflower and pumpkin seeds

some sage leaves

20 drops of damiana

Feed all the ingredients, except the damiana, into the juicer. Pour the juice into a glass and stir int9 he damiana. Makes approximately 350ml (just over 1¼ cups) of delicious juice.

Energy (kcal): 350 Protein: 14.5g Fat: 24.6g Saturated fat: 3.2g Monounsaturated fat: 5.5g Polyunsaturated fat: 12.8g Carbohydrates: 18.3g Total Sugars: 9.4g Dietary fibre: 5.9g Sodium: 44mg Potassium: 1,376mg Calcium: 142mg Magnesium: 195mg Phosphorus: 467mg Iron: 8.08mg Copper: 1.00mg Zinc: 3.6mg Selenium: 16.1µg Vitamin A: 424µg Beta-carotene: 2,546µg Vitamin B3: 4.11mg Vitamin B6: 0.39mg Vitamin B12: 0µg Folic Acid: 122µg Vitamin C: 108mg Vitamin E: 12.33mg.

Minty Fresh

A refreshing drink full of the vital B vitamins to restore you energy and nerves and so relieve stress and anxiety, the basil in Minty Fresh is known to have calming properties.

You could also try Blood Tonic (see page 61) or Avocado Cream (see page 73) which helps combat stress.

2 bananas, peeled and diced
½ cucumber, peeled and diced
1 apple, cored and diced
some fresh mint
some fresh basil
1 teaspoon bee pollen

Place all the ingredients in the blender and mix until smooth. Makes approximately 300ml (1¼ cups).

> **Energy (kcal): 119 Protein: 1.5g Fat: 0.4g**
> **Saturated fat: 0.1g Monounsaturated fat: 0.0g**
> **Polyunsaturated fat: 0.2g Carbohydrates: 29.2g**
> **Total Sugars: 26.8g Dietary fibre: 4.1g Sodium: 3mg Potassium: 467mg Calcium: 13mg**
> **Magnesium: 37mg Phosphorus: 35mg Iron: 0.50mg Copper: 0.11mg Zinc: 0.3mg Selenium: 1.0µg Vitamin A: 13µg Beta-carotene: 75µg**
> **Vitamin B3: 0.77mg Vitamin B6: 0.32mg Vitamin B12: 0µg Folic Acid: 16µg Vitamin C: 15mg**
> **Vitamin E: 0.61mg.**

Tall

If you suffer from fatigue, then this is the drink for you. The tomatoes and avocados are good sources of B vitamins as well as vitamin C and essential minerals, so you'll really be walking tall after drinking this.

1 avocado, peeled, stoned and diced
3 tomatoes, diced
dash of lemon juice
1 teaspoon bee pollen

Place all the ingredients in the blender and mix until smooth. Makes approximately 250ml (about a cup) of juice.

> **Energy (kcal): 176 Protein: 2.8g Fat: 15.2g**
> **Saturated fat: 3.3g Monounsaturated fat: 9.3g**
> **Polyunsaturated fat: 2.0g Carbohydrates: 7.6g**
> **Total Sugars: 6.5g Dietary fibre: 2.5g Sodium: 22mg Potassium: 832mg Calcium: 22mg**
> **Magnesium: 33mg Phosphorus: 76mg Iron: 1.28mg Copper: 0.16mg Zinc: 0.5mg Selenium: 0.1µg Vitamin A: 210µg Beta-carotene: 1,261µg**
> **Vitamin B3: 2.78mg Vitamin B6: 0.55mg Vitamin B12: 0µg Folic Acid: 42µg Vitamin C: 40mg**
> **Vitamin E: 4.78mg.**

Minty Fresh

Green Monster

Yes, you guessed correctly, this green drink is bursting with chlorophyll, which has been shown to build up red blood cells, and it's another drink that will provide you with instant but slow-released energy, as the sunflower seeds and almonds are a good source of essential fatty acids and B vitamins.

400g (14oz) spinach, thoroughy washed
1 teaspoon ground sunflower seeds
50g (2oz) of ground almonds
2 dates
200ml (about a cup) water

Feed the spinach into the juicer. Then pour the juice into a blender, add the rest of the ingredients and mix. Makes approximately 700ml (2¾ cups).

> **Energy (kcal): 498 Protein: 23.4g Fat: 32.9g**
> **Saturated fat: 0.6g Monounsaturated fat: 18.0g**
> **Polyunsaturated fat: 10.3g Carbohydrates: 28.2g**
> **Total Sugars: 25.8g Dietary fibre: 24.1g Sodium:**
> **570mg Potassium: 2,599mg Calcium: 818mg**
> **Magnesium: 376mg Phosphorus: 495mg Iron:**
> **10.48mg Copper: 0.81mg Zinc: 4.7mg Selenium:**
> **8.6µg Vitamin A: 2,359µg Beta-carotene:**
> **14,151µg Vitamin B3: 6.97mg Vitamin B6: 0.80mg**
> **Vitamin B12: 0µg Folic Acid: 627µg Vitamin C:**
> **104mg Vitamin E: 20.26mg.**

Volatile

If you're suffering from insomnia, then this is the drink for you. the lettuce contains natural sleep-inducing substances and together with fennel is calming to the nerves.

8 lettuce leaves, thoroughly washed
½ bulb of fennel
½ lemon
20 drops of brahmi

Feed the lettuce, fennel and lemon into the juicer. Pour the juice into a glass and stir in the brahmi drops. Makes approximately 300ml (1¼ cups) of juice.

> **Energy (kcal): 44 Protein: 2.9g Fat: 1.3g**
> **Saturated fat: 0.2g Monounsaturated fat: 0.0g**
> **Polyunsaturated fat: 0.7g Carbohydrates: 5.5g**
> **Total Sugars: 5.4g Dietary fibre: 2.3g Sodium:**
> **16mg Potassium: 961mg Calcium: 68mg**
> **Magnesium: 22mg Phosphorus: 85mg Iron:**
> **1.45mg Copper: 0.03mg Zinc: 1.0mg Selenium:**
> **2.0µg Vitamin A: 114µg Beta-carotene: 685µg**
> **Vitamin B3: 1.82mg Vitamin B6: 0.14mg Vitamin**
> **B12: 0µg Folic Acid: 151µg Vitamin C: 22mg**
> **Vitamin E: 1.0mg.**

Green Monster

Red or Dead

Another tasty tipple to help combat insomnia, Red or Dead contains many essential minerals, such as calcium, magnesium, iron, phosphorus, potassium and sodium. The vitamin A from the carrots helps to protect our immune system.

4 medium-sized carrots, topped and tailed
6 lettuce leaves, thoroughly washed
½ beetroot

Feed all the ingredients into the juicer and pour the juice into a glass. Makes approximately 250ml (1 cup) of juice.

> Energy (kcal): 75 Protein: 2.0g Fat: 1.0g
> Saturated fat: 0.2g Monounsaturated fat: 0.0g
> Polyunsaturated fat: 0.6g Carbohydrates: 15.3g
> Total Sugars: 14.4g Dietary fibre: 5.7g Sodium:
> 52mg Potassium: 510mg Calcium: 60mg
> Magnesium: 11mg Phosphorus: 56mg Iron:
> 1.12mg Copper: 0.04mg Zinc: 0.4mg Selenium:
> 2.4µg Vitamin A: 2,202µg Beta-carotene:
> 13,214µg Vitamin B3: 0.81mg Vitamin B6: 0.25mg
> Vitamin B12: 0µg Folic Acid: 88µg Vitamin C:
> 14mg Vitamin E: 1.34mg.

Funky Monkey

If you overindulged on the drinking front the night before, this makes a great treat for the day after. It contains the vital vitamins B1 and C and the mineral potassium to help your body expel the alcohol from your system.

½ cantaloupe melon, peeled and seeds
        removed
1 banana, peeled and diced
100ml (½ cup) coconut milk
some fresh mint

Place all the ingredients in the blender and mix until smooth. Makes approximately 450ml (2 cups).

> Energy (kcal): 427 Protein: 6.6g Fat: 24.9g
> Saturated fat: 22.3g Monounsaturated fat: 2g
> Polyunsaturated fat: 0.0g Carbohydrates: 46g
> Total Sugars: 38.4g Dietary fibre: 5.8g Sodium:
> 135mg Potassium: 1,315mg Calcium: 115mg
> Magnesium: 97mg Phosphorus: 198mg Iron:
> 3.08mg Copper: 0.14mg Zinc: 0.3mg Selenium:
> 1.0µg Vitamin A: 506µg Beta-carotene: 3,035µg
> Vitamin B3: 3.42mg Vitamin B6: 0.65mg Vitamin
> B12: 0µg Folic Acid: 31µg Vitamin C: 92mg
> Vitamin E: 0.66mg.

Funky Monkey

Headstrong

Great for relieving a headache or migraine, the celery in Headstrong contains potassium and sodium, which help to restore the body's fluid balance, while the fennel is calming to the nerves and contains some B vitamins, which provide energy.

1 stalk of celery
½ bulb of fennel
6 lettuce leaves, thoroughly washed
½ pineapple, peeled and cut into chunks
some lemon balm

Feed all the ingredients into the juicer, starting with the lemon balm and pineapple and pour the juice into a glass. Makes approximately 300ml (1¼ cups) of juice.

> Energy (kcal): 56 Protein: 1.9g Fat: 0.8g
> Saturated fat: 0.1g Monounsaturated fat: 0.1g
> Polyunsaturated fat: 0.4g Carbohydrates: 10.9g
> Total Sugars: 10.8g Dietary fibre: 2.8g Sodium:
> 36mg Potassium: 708mg Calcium: 64mg
> Magnesium: 25mg Phosphorus: 56mg Iron:
> 0.99mg Copper: 0.10mg Zinc: 0.6g Selenium:
> 2.1µg Vitamin A: 58µg Beta-carotene: 4347µg
> Vitamin B3: 1.20mg Vitamin B6: 0.14mg Vitamin
> B12: 0µg Folic Acid: 79µg Vitamin C: 20mg
> Vitamin E: 0.61mg.

Breathe Easy

Allergies are becoming more and more of a problem, so this tasty little drink provides vitamin C to give your immune system a boost plus beta-carotene, a powerful antioxidant, and B vitamins to calm the nerves.

100g (4oz) radishes
1 stalk of celery
1 red pepper, stalk removed and deseeded
1 medium parsnip, topped and tailed
50g (2oz) watercress
some parsley

Feed all the ingredients into the juicer. Makes approximately 400ml (just under 2 cups) of juice.

> Energy (kcal): 113 Protein: 5.1g Fat: 2.0g
> Saturated fat: 0.5g Monounsaturated fat: 0.2g
> Polyunsaturated fat: 0.8g Carbohydrates: 19.7g
> Total Sugars: 16.7g Dietary fibre: 8.6g Sodium:
> 75mg Potassium: 991mg Calcium: 157mg
> Magnesium: 51mg Phosphorus: 127mg Iron:
> 2.84mg Copper: 0.06mg Zinc: 0.9g Selenium:
> 4.1µg Vitamin A: 1,508µg Beta-carotene: 9,049µg
> Vitamin B3: 3.65mg Vitamin B6: 0.96mg Vitamin
> B12: 0µg Folic Acid: 121µg Vitamin C: 341mg
> Vitamin E: 2.80mg.

Veggie Garden

Just as the name insinuates, this is a truly green drink but with great flavour and great for fighting those allergies again. It contains an excellent amount of vitamin C and beta-carotene, the kale and broccoli contain cancer preventative properties and the carrots and pepper add some sweetness to this drink.

6 florets of broccoli
50g (2oz) kale, thoroughly washed
1 stalk of celery
3 medium-sized carrots, topped and tailed
½ red pepper, stalk removed and
      deseeded
a few drops of lemon juice

Feed the first five ingredients into the juicer and pour the juice into a glass and stir in the lemon juice. Makes approximately 320ml (just over 1¼ cups).

Energy (kcal): 150 Protein: 11.1g Fat: 3.2g
Saturated fat: 0.7g Monounsaturated fat: 0.2g
Polyunsaturated fat: 1.8g Carbohydrates: 20.1g
Total Sugars: 18.7g Dietary fibre: 7.4g Sodium:
96mg Potassium: 1,369mg Calcium: 217mg
Magnesium: 75mg Phosphorus: 228mg Iron:
4.59mg Copper: 0.09mg Zinc: 1.5mg Selenium:
3.6μg Vitamin A: 2,692μg Beta-carotene:
16,151μg Vitamin B3: 3.71mg Vitamin B6: 0.91mg
Vitamin B12: 0μg Folic Acid: 256μg Vitamin C:
356mg Vitamin E: 4.62mg.

Celebrate

High in essential minerals to top up the calcium needed to repair the damages caused by the inorganic calcium deposits which are a factor in arthritis, this great drink is a must if you suffer from any aches and pains. It also contains sodium and vitamin C which are beneficial too in removing these deposits.

2 lemons, halved
3 stalks of celery
1 teaspoon brown sugar
1 teaspoon spirulina powder

Feed the lemons and the celery into the juicer and pour the juice into a glass. Stir in the sugar and the spirulina. Makes approximately 200ml (½ a cup) of juice.

Energy (kcal): 34 Protein: 0.9g Fat: 0.3g
Saturated fat: 0.0g Monounsaturated fat: 0.0g
Polyunsaturated fat: 0.1g Carbohydrates: 7.7g
Total Sugars: 7.7g Dietary fibre: 2.2g Sodium:
83mg Potassium: 543mg Calcium: 64mg
Magnesium: 13mg Phosphorus: 35mg Iron:
0.71mg Copper: 0.04mg Zinc: 0.1mg Selenium:
4.8μg Vitamin A: 13μg Beta-carotene: 77μg
Vitamin B3: 0.49mg Vitamin B6: 0.08mg Vitamin
B12: 0μg Folic Acid: 32μg Vitamin C: 40mg
Vitamin E: 0.27mg.

Veggie Garden

Tutti Fruity

A brilliantly colourful drink bursting with healing beta-carotene and vitamin C to protect your body, Tutti Fruity can also alleviate some symptoms of allergies. Plus it tastes divine!

3 sharon fruit, peeled

2 passion fruit, peeled

1 pear, cored and diced

2 kiwis, peeled

2 apples, cored and diced

1 lemon, peeled, diced and pips removed

You may find it easier to cut the sharon fruit and the passion fruit in half and scoop out the flesh. Place all the ingredients in the blender and mix until smooth. Makes approximately 400ml (just under 2 cups).

Energy (kcal): 250 Protein: 3.7g Fat: 1.1g
Saturated fat: 0.0g Monounsaturated fat: 0.0g
Polyunsaturated fat: 0.2g Carbohydrates: 59.7g
Total Sugars: 59.3g Dietary fibre: 4.0g Sodium:
23mg Potassium: 1,015mg Calcium: 67mg
Magnesium: 54mg Phosphorus: 110mg Iron:
1.53mg Copper: 0.33mg Zinc: 0.8mg Selenium:
0.4µg Vitamin A: 58µg Beta-carotene: 348µg
Vitamin B3: 1.47mg Vitamin B6: 0.36mg Vitamin
B12: 0µg Folic Acid: 11µg Vitamin C: 117mg
Vitamin E: 2.23mg.

Wacky-Wacky

A lovely, sweet-tasting drink with a sharp kick due to the kiwi and grapefruit, Wacky-wacky can also help combat aches and pains. The grapefruit is very high in potassium and sodium as well as the vital vitamin C, so it helps to regulate the fluid balance in the body.

1 grapefruit, peeled, diced and pips removed

1 pomegranate, peeled

1 kiwi, peeled and diced

125g (5oz) white seedless grapes

Place all the ingredients in the blender and mix until smooth. Makes approximately 300ml (1¼ cups) of juice.

Energy (kcal): 160 Protein: 2.7g Fat: 0.6g
Saturated fat: 0.0g Monounsaturated fat: 0.0g
Polyunsaturated fat: 0.0g Carbohydrates: 38.1g
Total Sugars: 37.9g Dietary fibre: 3.5g Sodium:
10mg Potassium: 794mg Calcium: 70mg
Magnesium: 34mg Phosphorus: 79mg Iron:
0.90mg Copper: 0.29mg Zinc: 0.3mg Selenium:
2.8µg Vitamin A: 13µg Beta-carotene: 76µg
Vitamin B3: 0.96mg Vitamin B6: 0.32mg Vitamin
B12: 0µg Folic Acid: 44µg Vitamin C: 99mg
Vitamin E: 0.30mg.

Tutti Fruity

Kick Start

If you thought gout was thing of the past, think again. This great drink with its alkalising properties can help to rebalance the body's pH levels promoting secretion of the toxins which form crystals in the joints. It is full of beta-carotene and vitamin C plus calcium to help rebuild the damage caused.

You can also try Defuse (see page 53).

½ red pepper, stalk removed and
        deseeded
150g (6oz) spinach, thoroughly washed
½ cucumber
1 apple, quartered
5 Cos lettuce leaves, thoroughly washed

Feed all the ingredients into the juicer and pour the juice into a glass. Makes approximately 300ml (1¼ cups).

> Energy (kcal): 169 Protein: 7.9g Fat: 2.6g
> Saturated fat: 0.4g Monounsaturated fat: 0.2g
> Polyunsaturated fat: 1.5g Carbohydrates: 29.6g
> Total Sugars: 28.8g Dietary fibre: 13.2g Sodium:
> 225mg Potassium: 1,473mg Calcium: 307mg
> Magnesium: 126mg Phosphorus: 190mg Iron:
> 4.54mg Copper: 0.11mg Zinc: 1.6g Selenium:
> 2.2µg Vitamin A: 2,208µg Beta-carotene:
> 13,249µg Vitamin B3: 5.09mg Vitamin B6:
> 1.09mg Vitamin B12: 0µg Folic Acid: 313µg
> Vitamin C: 330mg Vitamin E: 5.20mg.

Go-Go

Full of necessary laxative fibres and benefiting from the properties of the pawpaw or papaya which help cleanse the kidneys, liver and intestine, Go-Go will give you relief from constipation.

½ pawpaw, peeled and diced
125g (5oz) white seedless grapes
1 apple, cored and diced
slice of peeled ginger

Place all ingredients in the blender and mix until smooth. If you find it too thick, add some still or sparkling water as you mix it. Makes about 300ml (1¼ cups).

> Energy (kcal): 128 Protein: 1.1g Fat: 0.3g
> Saturated fat: 0.0g Monounsaturated fat: 0.0g
> Polyunsaturated fat: 0.1g Carbohydrates: 32.4g
> Total Sugars: 32g Dietary fibre: 3.4g Sodium:
> 7mg Potassium: 427mg Calcium: 25mg
> Magnesium: 16mg Phosphorus: 35mg Iron:
> 0.62mg Copper: 0.18mg Zinc: 0.3mg Selenium:
> 1.2µg Vitamin A: 34µg Beta-carotene: 203µg
> Vitamin B3: 0.48mg Vitamin B6: 0.19mg Vitamin
> B12: 0µg Folic Acid: 4µg Vitamin C: 22mg
> Vitamin E: 0.59mg.

Go-Go

Wind Shield

A good drink to combat the often embarrassing problem of flatulence, Wind Shield provides the bowel with good dietary fibres and the fennel is a great soother with anti-inflammatory properties.

2 medium-sized carrots, topped and tailed
half an apple
½ beetroot
½ bulb of fennel

Feed all the ingredients into the juicer and pour the juice into a glass. Makes about 250ml (1 cup) of juice.

Energy (kcal): 73 Protein: 1.6g Fat: 0.4g
Saturated fat: 0.1g Monounsaturated fat: 0.0g
Polyunsaturated fat: 0.2g Carbohydrates: 16.6g
Total Sugars: 16.1g Dietary fibre: 3.9g Sodium:
40mg Potassium: 547mg Calcium: 41mg
Magnesium: 12mg Phosphorus: 44mg Iron:
0.66mg Copper: 0.04mg Zinc: 0.5mg Selenium:
0.8µg Vitamin A: 1,099µg Beta-carotene:
6,592µg Vitamin B3: 0.60mg Vitamin B6: 0.19mg
Vitamin B12: 0µg Folic Acid: 62µg Vitamin C:
13mg Vitamin E: 0.84mg.

Sunrise

A wonderfully refreshing drink which will help heal tummy if you are suffering from indigestion, the papaya in Sunrise contains an enzyme called papain that helps to break down protein and aids your stomach enzymes in the digestion of other foods.

½ papaya, peeled and diced
½ pineapple, peeled and diced
1 orange, peeled, diced and pips removed
30 white seedless grapes
1 pear, cored and diced

Place all the ingredients in the blender and mix until smooth. Makes approximately 500ml (2¼ cups).

Energy (kcal): 379 Protein: 5.2g Fat: 1.2g
Saturated fat: 0.0g Monounsaturated fat: 0.3g
Polyunsaturated fat: 0.3g Carbohydrates: 92g
Total Sugars: 85.4g Dietary fibre: 9.8g Sodium:
41mg Potassium: 1,571mg Calcium: 211mg
Magnesium: 158mg Phosphorus: 150mg Iron:
2.30mg Copper: 0.82mg Zinc: 1.1mg Selenium:
2.8µg Vitamin A: 28µg Beta-carotene: 169µg
Vitamin B3: 2.50mg Vitamin B6: 0.61mg Vitamin
B12: 0µg Folic Acid: 72µg Vitamin C: 178mg
Vitamin E: 1.75mg.

Sunrise

Classic Banana

Heartburn is another common problem, so the banana in this soothing drink will help by lining the walls of the oesophagus and stomach, thereby reducing acidity levels. In the meantime, the cinnamon warms the whole system.

1 banana, peeled and diced
150ml (⅔ cup) soya milk or semi-skimmed milk
a few drops of vanilla flavour
a pinch of cinnamon

Place all the ingredients in the blender and mix until smooth. Makes approximately 250ml (about a cup).

> **Energy (kcal): 164 Protein: 6.2g Fat:2.96g**
> **Saturated fat: 1.8g Monounsaturated fat: 0.8g**
> **Polyunsaturated fat: 0.1g Carbohydrates: 30.4g**
> **Total Sugars: 28.1g Dietary fibre: 3.1g Sodium:**
> **76mg Potassium: 634mg Calcium: 194mg**
> **Magnesium: 52mg Phosphorus: 164mg Iron:**
> **1.28mg Copper: 0.36mg Zinc: 0.8g Selenium:**
> **2.8μg Vitamin A: 67μg Beta-carotene: 40μg**
> **Vitamin B3: 0.87mg Vitamin B6: 0.36mg Vitamin**
> **B12: 0.3μg Folic Acid: 17μg Vitamin C: 11mg**
> **Vitamin E: 0.31mg. Calculations are based on**
> **skimmed milk.**

Easy

Another soothing drink, the ingredients in Easy help to encourage good bacteria in the stomach to counteract any acidity caused by heartburn.

½ bulb of fennel
75g (3oz) alfalfa
1 stalk of celery
140g (5oz) white grapes

Feed all the ingredients into the juicer, starting with the alfalfa and then pour the juice into a glass. This makes about 300ml (1¼ cups) of juice.

> **Energy (kcal): 99 Protein: 4.0g Fat: 0.8g**
> **Saturated fat: 0.0g Monounsaturated fat: 0.0g**
> **Polyunsaturated fat: 0.0g Carbohydrates: 20.2g**
> **Total Sugars: 20.1g Dietary fibre: 1.7g Sodium:**
> **40mg Potassium: 715mg Calcium: 71mg**
> **Magnesium: 34mg Phosphorus: 96mg Iron:**
> **1.42mg Copper: 0.27mg Zinc: 1.1mg Selenium:**
> **2.5μg Vitamin A: 32μg Beta-carotene: 194μg**
> **Vitamin B3: 1.09mg Vitamin B6: 0.19mg Vitamin**
> **B12: 0μg Folic Acid: 60μg Vitamin C: 12mg**
> **Vitamin E: 0.09mg.**

Classic Banana

Rice Dream

This drink alkalises and neutralises acidity in the stomach and so is excellent for alleviating gastritis. The yoghurt soothes inflammation and the apricots contain a natural painkiller.

Try also Avocado Cream (see page 73).

250ml (1 cup) rice milk
125g (5oz) low fat vanilla yoghurt with live
    cultures
6 dried apricots
a pinch of cinnamon

Place all the ingredients in the blender and mix until smooth. Makes approximately 350ml (just over 1¼ cups).

> Energy (kcal): 347 Protein: 7.9g Fat: 4.1g
> Saturated fat: 0.8g Monounsaturated fat: 0.9g
> Polyunsaturated fat: 1.8g Carbohydrates: 73.4g
> Total Sugars: 63.9g Dietary fibre: 13g Sodium:
> 115mg Potassium: 1,375mg Calcium: 566mg
> Magnesium: 59mg Phosphorus: 223mg Iron:
> 3.31mg Copper: 0.25mg Zinc: 1.1mg Selenium:
> 5.7μg Vitamin A: 76μg Beta-carotene: 397μg
> Vitamin B3: 1.95mg Vitamin B6: 0.19mg Vitamin
> B12: 1.7μg Folic Acid: 32μg Vitamin C: 1mg
> Vitamin E: 1.8μg.

Popeye

Maintaining balanced blood sugar levels is very important and Popeye helps do just that. It is rich in vitamins A and C, and also contains the essential minerals iron, calcium and magnesium.

100g (4oz) spinach, thoroughly washed
25g (1oz) watercress
4 kale leaves, thoroughly washed
1 apple, quartered
3 medium-sized carrots, topped and tailed
2 teaspoons ginseng powder

Feed all the ingredients, except for the ginseng, into the juicer and pour the juice into a glass. Stir in the ginseng. Makes approximately 300ml (1¼ cups) of juice.

> Energy (kcal): 140 Protein: 6.9g Fat: 2.5g
> Saturated fat: 0.4g Monounsaturated fat: 0.2g
> Polyunsaturated fat: 1.5g Carbohydrates: 23.8g
> Total Sugars: 23.1g Dietary fibre: 11.9g Sodium:
> 214mg Potassium: 1,163mg Calcium: 333mg
> Magnesium: 88mg Phosphorus: 126mg Iron:
> 4.24mg Copper: 0.10mg Zinc: 1.4mg Selenium:
> 3.4μg Vitamin A: 2,656μg Beta-carotene:
> 15,934μg Vitamin B3: 2.23mg Vitamin B6:
> 0.62mg Vitamin B12: 0μg Folic Acid: 237μg
> Vitamin C: 124mg Vitamin E: 4.43mg.

Popeye

Spring Clean

If you suffer from circulation problems, then you need to give your body a Spring Clean! (OK, groan if you want.) But this drink really helps your blood flow by dilating the blood vessels and it is rich in beta-carotene with all its antioxidant properties.

25g (1oz) watercress

100g (4oz) spinach, thoroughly washed

2 medium-sized carrots, topped and tailed

½ beetroot

20 drops of ginkgo biloba

Feed the first four ingredients into the juicer and pour into a glass. Stir in the ginkgo biloba drops. Makes approximately 250ml (1 cup) of juice.

> Energy (kcal): 66 Protein: 4.5g Fat: 1.4g
> Saturated fat: 0.3g Monounsaturated fat: 0.1g
> Polyunsaturated fat: 0.8g Carbohydrates: 9.4g
> Total Sugars: 8.8g Dietary fibre: 7.4g Sodium:
> 186mg Potassium: 772mg Calcium: 244mg
> Magnesium: 63mg Phosphorus: 82mg Iron:
> 3.17mg Copper: 0.06mg Zinc: 1.1mg Selenium:
> 1.8µg Vitamin A: 1,798µg Beta-carotene:
> 10,786µg Vitamin B3: 1.47mg Vitamin B6: 0.36mg
> Vitamin B12: 0µg Folic Acid: 186µg Vitamin C:
> 50mg Vitamin E: 2.60mg.

Pink Paradise

This great tasting drink is full of immune-boosting vitamin C and beta-carotene as well as essential minerals to keep blood cells supplied with oxygen. As such, it's very helpful in alleviating varicose veins.

½ mango, peeled and diced

1 sharon fruit, peeled and diced

10 raspberries

½ pink grapefruit, peeled and diced, pips
    removed

½ teaspoon vitamin C powder

1 teaspoon aloe vera juice

Place all the ingredients in the blender and mix until smooth. Makes approximately 500ml (2¼ cups).

> Energy (kcal): 149 Protein: 1.3g Fat: 0.3g
> Saturated fat: 0.1g Monounsaturated fat: 0.0g
> Polyunsaturated fat: 0.0g Carbohydrates: 11.1g
> Total Sugars: 11g Dietary fibre: 4.7g Sodium: 4mg
> Potassium: 247mg Calcium: 27mg Magnesium:
> 18mg Phosphorus: 30mg Iron: 0.6mg Copper:
> 0.10mg Zinc: 0.2mg Selenium: 0.5µg Vitamin A:
> 122µg Beta-carotene: 732µg Vitamin B3: 0.56mg
> Vitamin B6: 0.09mg Vitamin B12: 0µg Folic Acid:
> 27µg Vitamin C: 47mg Vitamin E: 0.71mg.

Pink Paradise

Oriental Cooler

Delightful and really fruity to the taste, Oriental Cooler also contains all the properties needed to reduce the pain of varicose veins.

½ pawpaw, peeled and diced
½ grapefruit, peeled, diced and pips removed
125g (5oz) red grapes
some mint
20 drops of ginkgo biloba

You could extract the juice of the grapefruit by using a citrus fruit, if you prefer. Otherwise place all the ingredients in the blender and mix until smooth. Make approximately 250ml (1 cup).

If you prefer, you can dilute this drink by adding some mineral water during blending.

Energy (kcal): 102 Protein: 1.1g Fat: 0.2g
Saturated fat: 0.0g Monounsaturated fat: 0.0g
Polyunsaturated fat: 0.0g Carbohydrates: 25.5g
Total Sugars: 25.4g Dietary fibre: 2.4g Sodium:
5mg Potassium: 425mg Calcium: 38mg
Magnesium: 16mg Phosphorus: 38mg Iron:
0.72mg Copper: 0.18mg Zinc: 0.2mg Selenium:
1.8µg Vitamin A: 35µg Beta-carotene: 207µg
Vitamin B3: 0.50mg Vitamin B6: 0.15mg Vitamin
B12: 0µg Folic Acid: 19µg Vitamin C: 36mg
Vitamin E: 0.20mg.

Sing

Singers have been known to use pineapple to soothe a sore throat and it really works, due to the enzyme bromelin that it contains. In addition, the salicylates found in the strawberries act as a natural painkiller and throat soother.

1 pineapple, peeled and diced
100g (4oz) strawberries
2 passion fruit, peeled

You could cut the passion fruit in half and scoop out the flesh if you prefer. Otherwise, place all the ingredients in the blender and mix until smooth. Makes approximately 500ml (2¼ cups).

Energy (kcal): 235 Protein: 3.5g Fat: 1.2g
Saturated fat: 0.0g Monounsaturated fat: 0.5g
Polyunsaturated fat: 0.5g Carbohydrates: 56.2g
Total Sugars: 56.2g Dietary fibre: 8.2g Sodium:
21mg Potassium: 988mg Calcium: 106mg
Magnesium: 96mg Phosphorus: 91mg Iron:
1.75mg Copper: 0.60mg Zinc: 0.8mg Selenium:
0µg Vitamin A: 53µg Beta-carotene: 319µg
Vitamin B3: 2.49mg Vitamin B6: 0.49mg Vitamin
B12: 0µg Folic Acid: 44µg Vitamin C: 142mg
Vitamin E: 0.68mg.

Sing

Bruiser

Some people bruise more easily than others, but this zingy little drink ensures the flow of blood to all body cells and helps remove any waste products, thereby encouraging repair in the damaged area. The enzyme bromelin present in pineapple can also help bruises, while the pink grapefruit is a good source of beta-carotene.

½ pineapple, peeled and diced
1 grapefruit, peeled, diced and pips removed

Place the ingredients in the blender and mix until smooth. You can dilute this drink with still or sparking water if you find it too thick. Makes approximately 250ml (1 cup).

Energy (kcal): 155 Protein: 1.9g Fat: 0.7g
Saturated fat: 0.0g Monounsaturated fat: 0.3g
Polyunsaturated fat: 0.3g Carbohydrates: 37.8g
Total Sugars: 37.8g Dietary fibre: 5.4g Sodium:
9mg Potassium: 672mg Calcium: 76mg
Magnesium: 58mg Phosphorus: 48mg Iron:
0.72mg Copper: 0.37mg Zinc: 0.3mg Selenium:
0.8μg Vitamin A: 12μg Beta-carotene: 71μg
Vitamin B3: 1.20mg Vitamin B6: 0.31mg Vitamin
B12: 0μg Folic Acid: 37μg Vitamin C: 67mg
Vitamin E: 0.47mg.

Saucy

As its name might imply, this delicious drink is good for stimulating the libido, packed as it is with the vitamins A and C and the minerals calcium, iron and sulphur.

2 medium-sized carrots, topped and tailed
4 cabbage leaves, thoroughy washed
1 stalk of celery
25g (1oz) coriander

Feed all the ingredients into a juicer, starting with the coriander and pour the juice into a glass.
Makes about 250ml (about a cup) of juice.

Energy (kcal): 68 Protein: 3.5g Fat: 1.0g
Saturated fat: 0.2g Monounsaturated fat: 0.0g
Polyunsaturated fat: 0.6g Carbohydrates: 12.2g
Total Sugars: 11.6g Dietary fibre: 6.3g Sodium:
61mg Potassium: 766mg Calcium: 130mg
Magnesium: 22mg Phosphorus: 81mg Iron:
1.83mg Copper: 0.07mg Zinc: 0.5mg Selenium:
3.3μg Vitamin A: 1,193μg Beta-carotene: 7,160μg
Vitamin B3: 1.11mg Vitamin B6: 0.38mg Vitamin
B12: 0μg Folic Acid: 112μg Vitamin C: 86mg
Vitamin E: 0.78mg.

Saucy

Magic

Another aphrodisiacal drink which is bursting with vitamins A and C and is high in sugars providing instant energy, Magic could just do the trick for you!

½ pawpaw, peeled and diced

3 dried figs

150g (6oz) red grapes

pinch of cinnamon

2 teaspoons guarana powder

Place all the ingredients in the blender and mix until smooth. Makes approximately 250ml (1 cup).

Energy (kcal): 233 Protein: 2.9g Fat: 1.2g
Saturated fat: 0.0g Monounsaturated fat: 0.0g
Polyunsaturated fat: 0.0g Carbohydrates: 56.6g
Total Sugars: 56.6g Dietary fibre: 9.1g Sodium:
42mg Potassium: 946mg Calcium: 197mg
Magnesium: 62mg Phosphorus: 84mg Iron:
3.79mg Copper: 0.38mg Zinc: 0.6mg Selenium:
1.8μg Vitamin A: 38μg Beta-carotene: 199μg
Vitamin B3: 0.86mg Vitamin B6: 0.31mg Vitamin
B12: 0μg Folic Acid: 9μg Vitamin C: 17mg Vitamin
E: 0mg.

Magic

Let Your Hair Down

The debate over the benefits or otherwise of alcohol still continues, but the drinks in this section all contain a dash of something which can enhance your mood and help you relax. However, they can be enjoyed without the alcohol and, if you are using the drinks as part of a detox programme, you should of course omit it.

Spicy Thai

A delicious sweet drink with a kick to it.

1 red pepper, stalk removed and deseeded
1 small red chilli pepper, stalk removed and deseeded
2 medium-sized carrots, topped and tailed
1 orange, quartered
1 measure of vodka
some crushed ice

Feed all the ingredients, except the vodka and the ice, into the juicer. Then mix the juice with the vodka and crushed ice in a glass. Makes approximately 450ml (2 cups) of juice.

Energy (kcal): 214 Alcohol: 8g Protein: 4.7g Fat: 1.3g Saturated fat: 0.3g Monounsaturated fat: 0.0g Polyunsaturated fat: 0.6g Carbohydrates: 33.4g Total Sugars: 31.7g Dietary fibre: 8.8g Sodium: 38mg Potassium: 782mg Calcium: 117mg Magnesium: 48mg Phosphorus: 90mg Iron: 1.24mg Copper: 0.12mg Zinc: 0.5mg Selenium: 2.4µg Vitamin A: 2,443µg Beta-carotene: 14,659µg Vitamin B3: 3.57mg Vitamin B6: 0.99mg Vitamin B12: 0µg Folic Acid: 102µg Vitamin C: 378mg Vitamin E: 2.43mg.

Spicy Thai

Bloody Red Mary

A lovely bright red drink which is full of vitamins A and C and beta-carotene.

1 apple, quartered
1 yellow pepper, stalk removed and deseeded
1 red pepper, stalk removed and deseeded
3 medium-sized carrots, topped and tailed
1 measure of vodka
some crushed ice

Feed all the ingredients, except the vodka and the crushed ice, into the juicer. Then mix the juice with the vodka and the ice in a glass and enjoy. Makes approximately 400ml (just under than 2 cups).

Energy (kcal): 260 Alcohol: 8g Protein: 5.5g Fat: 1.7g Saturated fat: 0.3g Monounsaturated fat: 0.0g Polyunsaturated fat: 0.9g Carbohydrates: 44.7g Total Sugars: 43.1g Dietary fibre: 12.9g Sodium: 49mg Potassium: 1,084mg Calcium: 66mg Magnesium: 69mg Phosphorus: 125mg Iron: 1.86mg Copper: 0.10mg Zinc: 0.6mg Selenium: 1.2µg Vitamin A: 2,968µg Beta-carotene: 17,806µg Vitamin B3: 4.34mg Vitamin B6: 1.61mg Vitamin B12: 0µg Folic Acid: 115µg Vitamin C: 553mg Vitamin E: 4.46mg.

Coffee Fantasy

A delicious alternative to the usual coffee that's drunk, Coffee Fantasy benefits from the liver-stimulating phytochemicals present in the dandelion as well as other essential minerals.

1 tablespoon ground dandelion coffee
boiling water
1 teaspoon of cream
1 measure of whisky or dark rum, as you
        prefer

Put the ground dandelion coffee in a cup and pour in the boiling water, add the cream and whisky or dark rum and stir.

Energy (kcal): 95 Alcohol: 8g Protein: 0.5g Fat: 3.8g Saturated fat: 2.4g Monounsaturated fat: 1.1g Polyunsaturated fat: 0.1g Carbohydrates: 0.8g Total Sugars: 0.8g Dietary fibre: 0g Sodium: 10mg Potassium: 24mg Calcium: 18mg Magnesium: 2mg Phosphorus: 15mg Iron: 0.02mg Copper: 0.0mg Zinc: 0.1mg Selenium: 0μg Vitamin A: 130μg Beta-carotene: 25μg Vitamin B3: 0.02mg Vitamin B6: 0.01mg Vitamin B12: 0μg Folic Acid: 1μg Vitamin C: 0mg Vitamin E: 0.08mg.

Coco Colada

The pineapple in this delicious drink will help the digestive processes and that and the lime are good sources of vitamin C.

1 pineapple, peeled and diced
100ml (half a cup) coconut milk
½ lime, peeled
measure of white rum
crushed ice

Place all the ingredients, except the crushed ice, in the blender and mix until smooth. Pour the smoothy into a glass and stir in the crushed ice. Makes approximately 750ml (3 cups).

Energy (kcal): 594 Alcohol: 8g Protein: 6.2g Fat: 26.6g Saturated fat: 22.2g Monounsaturated fat: 2.6g Polyunsaturated fat: 0.0g Carbohydrates: 75g Total Sugars: 75g Dietary fibre: 8.3g Sodium: 123mg Potassium: 1,339mg Calcium: 166mg Magnesium: 135mg Phosphorus: 99mg Iron: 3.09mg Copper: 0.76mg Zinc: 0.8mg Selenium: 0μg Vitamin A: 20μg Beta-carotene: 118μg Vitamin B3: 2.15mg Vitamin B6: 0.63mg Vitamin B12: 0μg Folic Acid: 34μg Vitamin C: 93mg Vitamin E: 0.64mg.

Coffee Fantasy

Conditions and Juices to take

Condition	Juice	Effect
Acne	The Kid p41 Radiance p43 Summer Time p43	Vitamin A and beta-carotene are essential for skin, hair and nails. The minerals potassium and sodium facilitate secretion of waste through the kidneys rather than the skin.
Anaemia	Blood Tonic p61 Powerful Greens p62	Packed with the essential minerals iron and folic acid to get you back on track.
Anxiety	Avocado Cream p73 Minty Fresh p91	Contains essential B vitamins for the energy and nerves topped with calming basil.
Arthritis	Celebrate p99 Green Living p89 Wacky-Wacky p101	High in essential minerals to top up calcium levels needed for repair. Sodium and vitamin C help to remove inorganic calcium deposits from the joints.
Asthma	Breath Easy p97 Veggie Garden p99 Tutti Fruity p101	These high-powered vitamin C drinks boost the immune system. The beta-carotene in them is a powerful antioxidant and the properties of the B vitamins have a calming effect.
Bad breath	All-Rounder p51	Causes can be many but the beta-carotene and vitamin C help the immune system, as well as fighting infection. Parsley helps cleanse the system.
Blood sugar	Popeye p109	Rich in vitamins A and C, contains essential iron, calcium and magnesium, and releases energy slowly to help maintain balanced blood sugar levels

Condition	Juice	Effect
Boils	Silky Too p45 Blood Red p45	High in Vitamin A and vital beta-carotene. These cleanse the liver and together with the minerals potassium, phosphorus and sodium aid secretion of waste via the kidneys and not the skin.
Broken bones	All-Rounder p51	Contains essential bone-building calcium and magnesium, which together with vitamin C aid the healing process
Bronchitis	Hot Stuff p87 Respirator p83	Has vitamin C to boost the immune system and a soothing and antibacterial action.
Bruising	Bruiser p115 Pink Paradise p111	Ensures the flow of blood to remove any waste. Aloe vera and vitamin C have healing properties
Catarrh	Red Devil p85	Has decongestant properties, gives a steady oxygen supply to the blood to protect the mucous membrane
Cholesterol	Replenish p57 Delightful p71	Reduces cholesterol, stimulating the urinary system to flush out waste.
Chronic fatigue	Green Monster p93 Tall p91	Provides instant energy, and also contains essential minerals and vitamins
Circulation weakness	Spring Clean p111	Aids in the flow of blood by dilating the blood vessels and improving circulation
Colds	Rocky p83 Immune Booster p81	Vitamin C boosts the immune system while echinacea is a herb known for its immune-strengthening properties

Condition	Juice	Effect
Constipation	Go-Go p103 Cool Mint p67	Provides laxative fibres as well as stimulating the kidneys to flush out waste.
Cough	Mint Apple p85 Grease Lightning p49	Soothing antibacterial and immune boosting action.
Cramp	Funky Monkey p95 Potassium Loader p67	Promotes the circulation and the high potassium content in both drinks is a good cramp preventative
Cystitis	Razzleberry p51	Antibacterial action, especially against bacteria causing cystitis
Dandruff	Pick Me Up p49	Rich in vitamins A, C and E and betacarotene as antioxidants and the B vitamins aid in normal cell production
Depression	Ruby Red p89	Full of essential B vitamins to help the nervous system and energy levels. Sage is calming and stimulating to the nervous system.
Diarrhoea	Berry Mania p70	Replenish body fluids, soothing and antibacterial properties
Eczema	Antioxidant p47	Essential vitamins A and E to promote healing of the skin
Energy	Caramba p55, Breakie p57, Tomato Punch p39, Full Of It p59, Replenish p57, Berry Mania p70	Gives a boost of energy, and is full of vitamins B, C and E as well as betacarotene.

Condition	Juice	Effect
Eyes	Tomato Punch p39 Thai Kick p41	Full of betacarotene, and vitamins A, B complex, C and E.
Fever	Free Falling p79 Delirious p81	Contains anti-inflammatory enzymes plus lots of vitamin C from citrus fruits.
Flatulence	Wind Shield p105	Fennel has essential anti-inflammatory properties, as well as providing the bowel with fibre.
Fluid retention	Cool Mint p67 Summer Time p43 Potassium Loader p67	Full of potassium to maintain sodium balance and has diuretic properties
Gastritis	Avocado Cream p73 Rice Dream p109	Neutralises stomach acidity with its alkaline properties and promotes digestion. Yoghurt soothes the inflammation and apricots contain salicylates, anti-flammatory compounds.
Gout	Kick Start p103 Defuse p53	Its alkaline properties help to rebalance ph levels promoting secretion of toxins. Calcium helps to repair damages to joints
Hair Problems	Shiny p47 Grease Lightning p49	Vitamins C and E, plus iron, silicon and sulphur are all good food for hair growth.
Hangover	Tropical Beach p70 Funky Monkey p95	Rehydrates the body and delivers vital potassium to regulate the water balance while the extra vitamin C boosts the immune system
Hay fever	Tutti Fruity p101 Veggie Garden p99	Both drinks are packed with essential vitamin C to protect the body.

Condition	Juice	Effect
Headache	Volatile p93 Headstrong p97	The high potassium and sodium content regulate the water balance, plus the vitamin B calms the nerves. Lemon balm has anti-spasmodic and soothing properties.
Heartburn	Classic Banana p107 Easy p107	Soothing and nourishing for good bacteria in the stomach.
Impotence	Iron Man p69	High in essential vitamin E, betacarotene and essential minerals to improve function.
Indigestion	Diamond White p71 Sunrise p105	An immune system booster, it also has soothing anti-bacterial properties.
Influenza	Caramba p55 Rocky p83	Contain masses of vitamin C and betacarotene.
Insomnia	Volatile p93 Red or Dead p95	A natural sleep-inducing substance is found in lettuce and they contains masses of vitamin C
Menopause	Breakie p57	Provides essential energy from the B vitamins as well as soothing nerves
Menstrual problems	Fragile p62 Femme Fatale p65	Soothing and anti-spasmodic, the flaxseed oil provides essential fatty acids to regulate the cycle.
Motion, morning sickness	Peachy p63 Groovy Chick p63	Ginger is known to help prevent motion and morning sickness.
Nails	Razzleberry p51 Defuse p53	Both drinks provide essential vitamins A, C and E plus betacarotene and the minerals iron, calcium, manganese and bioflavonoids.

Condition	Juice	Effect
Pregnancy	Caramba p55 Tropicana p65 Replenish p57	High in B vitamins, essential bone-building minerals and vitamins C and E, plus betacarotene with its strong antioxidant properties
Prostate problems	Ready Steady p69	Cleanses the prostate and reproductive glands
Rheumatism	Antioxidant p47 Razzleberry p51	Cleanses the body's systems, contain essential minerals and vitamin C
Sinusitis	Hot Stuff p87	Cleansing and beneficial to the sinuses and lungs
Skin	Radiance p43 Blood Red p45	High in betacarotene, essential skin minerals and healing vitamin C
Sore throat	Green Living p89 Sing p113	Soothing, sedative lettuce and cooling cucumber in the Gree Living. Bromelin and salicylates in Sing provide a natural painkiller and throat soother.
Stomach ulcers	Delightful p71 Tropicana p65	High in healing vitamin C and essential bioflavonoids
Stress	Blood Tonic p61	Cleanses with healing vitamin C and essential minerals
Tonsillitis	Sing p113	Contains healing enzyme bromelin and vitamin C
Varicose veins	Pink Paradise p111 Oriental Cooler p113	High in vitamin C and betacarotene to help the immune system plus essential minerals to keep the blood cells supplied with oxygen.

Equipment

Getting the right equipment for juicing is very important. You want a juicer that extracts the maximum amount of liquid from the fruit and vegetables, leaving you with dry pulp. There are many different kinds on the market and they vary considerably in quality and price.

Functionality and other factors are also important when deciding on what kind of juicer to buy. The easier it is to use and clean, the more often will you use your juicer. A good juicer will normally come with a warranty of 5–10 years, the less expensive juicers will only be guaranteed for up to a year. You should also consider how easy it is to find replacement parts – lesser known brands will probably be harder to get replacement parts for. Remember, too, that the quality of the juice extracted, in terms of the nutrient content, can vary depending on what extraction process is used.

Centrifugal

This juicer uses a grater or cutting disc to break up food and throws the fibres against a spinning basket, which separates the juice from the fibre. Oxygen is introduced during this process causing oxidation, which depletes nutrients over time, so it is important to consume the juice as soon as possible.

The centrifugal juicer is at the cheaper end of the market, ranging from £29–250 ($40–350). The most common brands available in good department stores are Waring, Magimix and Kenwood.

Masticator

Masticating juicers work by grinding the fruit and vegetables into smaller parts, which are forced against a screen extracting the juice, and the remaining pulp is ejected through an opening. This kind of action is far more efficient than that of the centrifugal juicers but these juicers are also more expensive, ranging from £300–400 ($420–560). They can also chop ice, make ice cream and nut and seed butters. Among the best known is the Champion Juicer.

Hydraulic Press

This is the ultimate juicer and is mainly used in commercial operations. It combines a grinder and hydraulic press, which allows for the maximum extraction of all nutrients. They have a very long life span but are also very expensive, up to $2000, and are not available in the UK.

Blenders

Blenders have a stainless steel cutting blade, which rotates at very high speeds. The fibres of the fruit or vegetables are retained within making drinks much thicker. They are ideal for making smoothies, cocktails, soups and baby foods. There are many different brands on the market ranging in price from £29–139 ($40–200), so there's something to suit everybody. Many brands are available on the market, such as Waring, Magimix Le Duo, Krups, Moulinex and Braun to name but a few.